Praise for the *Feng Shui Handbook for Real Estate Agents*

"This book delivers practical tools and spiritual insights that can be implemented immediately to improve your real estate results. Barbara Harwell's techniques have worked for my properties ever since I first met her in 2001!"

---Stefan Kasian, N.D., Ph.D., Real Estate Revolutionary and Doctor of Naturopathic Medicine & Transpersonal Psychology

"Feng Shui for real estate combined with clearing emotional energy makes for an interesting mix! As we understand energy better we see how we can impact our homes and our livelihoods for greater success and better health."

--Dr Bradley Nelson, DC (retired), Developer of The Emotion Code and Body Code Systems, *The Emotion Code* Author

"What an ideal marriage of tools, processes, and strategies that uses the knowledge of Feng Shui and energy to get that house SOLD. Barbara shares her knowledge of Feng Shui, Real Estate, Law of Attraction and more."

--Michael J Losier, NLP Practitioner and Author, *Law of Attraction*

Feng Shui Handbook
for Real Estate Agents

The Definitive Guide for Implementing
Powerful Secrets That Yield Quick Results

By Master Barbara Harwell, REALTOR®
and Master Denise Liotta Dennis

Ω
Moon Gate Press
Houston, Texas USA

Feng Shui Handbook for Real Estate Agents
*The Definitive Guide for Implementing Powerful Secrets
That Yield Quick Results*

Photography & Illustrations
Illustrations and charts created by Denise Liotta Dennis and Barbara Harwell. Home floor plans courtesy of Chesmar Homes. Thanks to the following photographers, some of whom are from Pixabay, Piqsels, Unsplash, Peakpx, Wikipedia Commons, PickPic, All Creative Commons, and FreestockPhotos.biz: Sergey Norkov, Kayla Maurais, Monicore, Hans, MonikaP, KarinKarin, TerimkasihO, Barbara Harwell, Devanath, Souljourney, Petr Kratochvil, Jack87, Magicbowls, Anaterate, Paulbr75, Vivenvivo, KoalaParkLaundrmat, Paulbr75, Koratge, Eilis Garvey, Connoman, Scott Lorsch, Avi Waxman, Engin_Akyurt, and StockSnap.

Book cover and book interior design by Denise Liotta-Dennis and Barbara Harwell. Cover photo taken by Saddleroad (Pixabay) and enhanced by Faizan2cool at Fiverr. Editors: Bonnie Lowery, Linda L. Dennis, REALTOR®, and Forrest Ann Ferguson.

ISBN: 9781704068367
Published in the United States of America
Published by Moon Gate Press and KDP

This book is dedicated to my parents
Walter and Jo Harwell

who transitioned while I was in my early twenties.
Thank you for being the wind beneath my wings.

Table of Contents

Acknowledgements

When reflecting on my journey I am astonished to realize how many magnificent people I am blessed to have in my life. There are those who have seemingly stopped by for a moment in time and those who have remained close even when separated by time and distance. Each holds a special place in my heart and life...now and always.

My precious parents, to whom this book is dedicated, I thank them in spirit for their unconditional love, trust and acceptance. They taught me to trust myself...quite frankly when I may not have been worthy of their trust. Yet, on those occasions I knew that I must rise to the occasion and make them proud. They shared an unshakeable faith in God that is my constant guidepost and my strong foundation now based on personal experience.

The guidance of two exceptional Feng Shui teachers is among my most precious gifts. My gratitude to Grandmaster Lillian Too, in Kuala Lumpur, Malaysia for her ability to make the complex study of Feng Shui so captivating and practical. Eternal gratitude to Master Denise Liotta Dennis for co-authoring this series of real estate Feng Shui books and challenging me deeper into the understanding of Feng Shui than I could have ever imagined possible. Thank you to my cherished friend, Master Marianne Kulekowskis, for introducing me to Denise.

Much gratitude to my wonderful mentors and teachers, Evangelist Rideout, Tony Robbins, Dr. Oscar Thompson, Michael J. Losier, S. Carl Friedsam JD, Brian Foster JD, Dr. Rhibi Kalla, Dr. Brad and Jean Nelson.

To my amazing children, Forrest Ann, Christian Dawn, Zack and Kim Michele, I offer my gratitude and appreciation for all their love and encouragement. Special love to my grandchildren, Christopher, Blake, Natalie, Hannah, Jack, Miriam, Josh, Nathanael and Gabriel.

Great appreciation for my clients, associates and friends who have provided the impetus to keep learning and growing in wisdom, knowledge and understanding...you are my treasures and I am forever grateful to you. You know who you are.

Special thanks to the "Magnificent Monahans 7" who are my lifelong friends and support system, Connie Ramsey Hisel, Loretta Williams Shumway, Patricia Paylor Davis, Sharon Fletcher Spurgin, Candy Mermis Kinsey and Patsy Carr Kleck.

To those friends who were instant connections and have been there for me through thick and thin...my soul family, Dr. Victoria and Marlan Gamber, Dr. Deborah Vogele Welch, Bonnie Lowery, Dr. Stefan Kasian, Claudia King, Debbie and David Johnstone, Jesse Arnold, Connie Wardman, Eric Carlyle, Melanie McMullin, Veronica Medina and Paty Morgan.

And to each of you, my new connections, I know you will realize through the following pages that real estate, Feng Shui and divine healing are my passions and legacy. I pray that everyone who experiences this book will be inspired, encouraged, enlightened and empowered.

Barbara Harwell, Feng Shui Master

A special thanks to our non-human assistants who delight our hearts with their love, loyalty and companionship.

Molly, *Barbara's Assistant*   CoCo, *Denise's Assistant*

Introduction

"The best investment on earth is earth."
--Louis Glickman

It has been a long-time desire for us to help homeowners and their real estate agents find superior homes and share strategies to sell homes quickly. So, this book was born out of a real need. You've heard the saying *"That information is on a need to know basis"*. Well, we believe you need to know!

There are essentially two types of Feng Shui:

Classical or traditional Feng Shui can be traced back 3,000 to 5,000 years and has complex formulas that were verbally passed from master to student until quite recently.

Western or contemporary (e.g. Black Hat Tibetan) which is a couple of hundred years old, new to the West within the past 30 years and is deeply rooted in Buddhism.

You probably remember the first time you heard the term Feng Shui (pronounced *fung shway)*. Your understanding of it was quite likely that it was some sort of design and placement of furniture and décor to create a harmonious environment.

Aahhh, but it is so much more.

Initially, it may have intrigued you. And if you did any research on the subject, you may have become even more confused than when you first learned how to pronounce the name. Every magazine article and book seemed to have a different perspective and conflicting information.

We are here to simplify that process and amplify good Feng Shui results. Since this is the main purpose of *Feng Shui Handbook for Real Estate Agents* it is important to understand there are different types of Feng Shui.

Barbara, one of the authors, was initially trained in Western Feng Shui and migrated to Classical Feng Shui in 2004. The following related story is the reason why.

"My business partner had recently moved from Belgium to the U.K. due to a job promotion. After moving into his new residence, he called and said something was very wrong. Since his move, he was required to travel around the world almost weekly and it was taking a heavy toll on his health. He asked me to see if there was something wrong with the Feng Shui, and if so, could it be adjusted.

He faxed me the floor plan, I analyzed the property and could not discern the problem based on Black Hat Feng Shui. Since I had recently discovered Lillian Too's Classical Feng Shui books and had been devouring them, I asked him to give me some time to see if I could find the problem by using the new formulas and techniques I had been learning. I then asked him to use a compass and take the home facing direction as well as the front entry direction. They were the same, thank goodness! This made it so much easier for me to analyze.

Almost instantly I could see the issue and knew he needed some earth (mountain) energy to anchor an area in the home. I gathered a large group of rocks from Arizona that he would be able to stack at least 3 feet tall and sent them Next Day FedEx. I included instructions as where to place them, how tall to stack them and intentions to verbally state while doing so.

Within a week, his travel schedule returned to normal and his good health was quickly restored. From that time on, he referred to Feng Shui as the 'Box of Rocks Theory.' For me, it was an awakening to a resource more powerful than I had ever experienced in the practice of Western Feng Shui."

This book is intended to be just that simple! We will guide you, step-by-step, with solutions that will bring property buying and selling to a new, exciting level. Classical Feng Shui can deliver the results that you and your clients want to experience.

In Chapter 1 you will learn how Feng Shui, a Chinese practice, became a worldwide phenomenon. Chapter 2 we will show you how to identify good homes to buy, rent or sell. The Good, Bad and Ugly addressed in Chapter 3 will show you where to focus your energies for the best results.

You will be guided in Chapters 4, 5 and 6 step-by-step to extract the best energy. Since this style of Feng Shui is more scientific, you will need to gather critical information about the property before proceeding with our recommendations in the *To Do List* sections. No worries just grab your smartphone and you are on your way! Additionally, we have created checklists to streamline the process. These three chapters are the essential keys to unlock powerful results. To our knowledge this is the only book on Feng Shui and real estate that has given such clear, concise directions on how to Feng Shui a house for successful buying and selling!

Chapter 7 addresses the issue of stagnate or negative energy in a home. This is a common issue that is often overlooked and it can impede the sale of a property. It is also useful when moving into a new home to clear the previous residents' energy.

You will find affirmations in Chapter 8 for you and your clients. These affirmations and prayers will accelerate either selling a home or finding that ideal property. Affirmations for investors are also included.

The Law of Attraction method is reviewed in Chapter 9. While this has been popular for many years, we give you some subtle nuances so it can work more powerfully. Chapter 10 is all about addressing the emotions that may be creating blocks to success. *The Emotion Code®* created by Dr. Bradley Nelson has helped millions of people worldwide do just that! In Chapter 11, we wrap it all up for professional real estate agents with helpful checklists. Remember to take a look at the Bonus Chapter where you will glimpse the depth of Classical Feng Shui techniques and methods used by masters.

Before you implement any changes it is best to read through the book at least once. This will give you the big picture and help you understand the process. Remember, this is a handbook designed to use again and again.

We are so pleased and excited to bring you this timely book. We know that whether you use this information for yourself, your clients, family or friends, you are on your way to a life with more prosperity, good health, harmony and loving relationships!

May You Be Blessed All the Days of Your Life!
Barbara and Denise

NOTE: We have capitalized the eight directions throughout the book due to their importance in Feng Shui. In many places we have abbreviated the intercardinal directions such as NE, SE, SW, NW for conciseness. There are common measurements that are used throughout the book and below is a table converting those U.S. customary units to metric system measurements.

U.S. Customary Units	Metric System
3 feet	.9144 meters
6 feet	1.8288 meters
8 feet	2.4384 meters

1

The Worldwide Phenomenon of Feng Shui

It has been about 25 years since real estate agents in the U.S. first started hearing about the practice of Feng Shui. Now it has reached global proportions.

Since the introduction of Feng Shui to the West, agents have tried to reconcile this Chinese method and its place in the real estate business. So, how did Feng Shui gain its popularity in the West all those years ago? With the passing of that much time, you may be wondering if you missed the boat, or if you arrived in the nick of time. Let us find out.

As you may know, China has given the world many gifts such as printing, the umbrella, compass, acupuncture, martial arts and of course, Feng Shui. Recent events, including coronavirus 19 may have created some prejudice against China.

The Chinese people have often suffered cruel and heavy-handed government rule throughout their 6,000-year history. This treatment has been from ancient royal dynasties as well as recent dictators. While the Chinese Communist Party (CCP) has committed many crimes against humanity, the general civilian population has not. For example, in the 2019-2020 Hong Kong riots we witnessed sincere cries for help as they protested the CCP infringement of their civil liberties.

Figure 1: Hong Kong is the "unofficial" capital of Classical Feng Shui.

During this long history, Feng Shui has fallen in and out of favor. At times it was even forbidden because the elite were aware of its potential to subdue their inequitable rule.

Articles began showing up in professional real estate magazines, guest speakers appeared at conferences, and Feng Shui training was gradually gearing toward realtors. Why? What supported the sudden popularity and acceptance of Feng Shui in real estate? Many agents heard about it through their Asian clients and investors, while others wanted to see if a home would sell faster by using it. Still others were just curious and did not want to be left out just in case it had some merit. The majority wrote it off as superstition, a cult or religious practice, and something that was not for them. Many agents thought Feng Shui was no different than home staging or interior design—what was all the hype about?

Sure, Feng Shui is a buzz word that has been on numerous forms of media – *HGTV, YouTube, Gaia, Dateline*, and many others. Yes, lots of movie stars, millionaires, billionaires, and corporations use it and tout its benefits. So what?! Unfortunately, when something becomes popular, inevitably there is a feeding frenzy of misinformation. The goal of this book is to provide you facts and solutions rather than getting caught up in the press and hype about Feng Shui.

Why are people so confused about Feng Shui? First of all, it is not common knowledge that there are two types of Feng Shui, Western and Classical. What? It is true and they are worlds apart. Okay great, but what is Feng Shui, exactly?

Simply put, Feng Shui is an ancient Chinese science that evaluates the quality of energy in a building or home. The purpose is to determine if it supports wealth, good health, and relationships. If not, alter it. This is achieved by spatial arrangement, floor plan design, and addressing energies, as described in this handbook.

While you will not be able to alter the design of the home, you will be able to arrange the space, cure negative energy, and enhance the best energy. When this takes place, a whole new harmonic frequency occurs. Now the home can 'broadcast' a new message and signal/attract buyers. On the other side, buyers will know what to look for, and look out for, when making this all-important investment.

Feng Shui Handbook for Real Estate Agents is the first book to evaluate properties through Feng Shui eyes with procedures identified for easy implementation. You will need to gather a few key pieces of information and then start the process.

As Feng Shui masters, we have created a concise, simple system in which agents can get the fastest results with minimum effort. That is the purpose and inspiration behind this groundbreaking book. We have designed checklists to gather information including a Step-by-Step Feng Shui Guide and a To-Do List for your client's unique home.

This book will totally clear up what Feng Shui is and is not. You will learn about Feng Shui methods and techniques used by Asian masters for thousands of years – methods and techniques that 95% of Feng Shui books do not even mention. Finally, you will understand how Feng Shui is used in our modern world, how to help yourself, your clients, friends, and family members achieve a better, more harmonious life.

It is fascinating how a Chinese practice has become so well-known and, for the most part, widely accepted by Americans. Feng Shui was first used to select an ideal burial site, and then to design and build cities, temples and homes.

In ancient and modern times, Feng Shui has been about living in harmony with the natural world/environment. For centuries, the Chinese culture has relied on Feng Shui concerning the essential aspects of life. Even today, Feng Shui is part of everyday life in Chinese populous countries and cities such as Singapore, Hong Kong, Taiwan, and Malaysia.

The Chinese believe there are three types of luck!

Heaven Luck

This is a gift that is bestowed to you at birth and is from Heaven.

Human Luck

This is the type of luck you make for yourself with education, focus, determination, effort and virtues.

Earth Luck

This is the realm of Feng Shui and the benefits derived from creating or having a supportive environment.

The Feng Shui phenomenon has now found its place all over the world and is embraced by all who have come to appreciate its benefit and practicality. In North America, where it was made so hugely popular, architects, real estate agents, interior designers, builders, developers, and homeowners became interested in Feng Shui, and quickly recognized its benefits.

Feng Shui dates back to antiquity. It is both an art and science that was born from experience and common sense. It is a skill to correct disharmony in the environment and improve our immediate living and working space. Since the discovery of quantum physics and the understanding that everything consists of energy, it is not surprising that people all over the world are now beginning to appreciate the science behind Feng Shui.

It took thousands of years to develop Feng Shui into a systematic, practical science. It is deeply rooted in the principles of the Tao. The famous *Tao Te Ching* is a Chinese classic text traditionally credited to the 6th century BC sage, Lao Zi. The ancients viewed the Earth and Universe as having yin and yang energy. Additionally, they categorized all things into five elements (wood, fire, earth, metal, and water).

As a technique for living, Feng Shui is best understood as the science of selecting and arranging a living space where the five elements and yin/yang energies are in complete balance whereby the occupants can enjoy a good life--prosperous and healthy!

While this may sound simple, in the world of Classical Feng Shui, it does take time to fully master these principles. This book has done the work for you by critiquing the homes and making the necessary recommendations.

Feng Shui retains certain mysticism. Acceptance of fundamental theories and beliefs about the Universe is required. These may appear to be rather foreign in the context of the modern world. For example, there are metaphors, and mythical Chinese references to animals, elements, and the invisible forces of yin and yang energy that, at first glance, may seem alien.

Nevertheless, its continued growth and popularity may be viewed as a tribute that it really works. Once you use and practice Feng Shui, you will develop a sensitivity and increased awareness of your environment. In other words, you will begin to develop an 'eye' for Feng Shui.

Some people mistakenly think that Feng Shui is a superstition. It is not. When the formulas and methods described in this book are implemented along with your positive intentions, you will observe quantum physics and seeming miracles in action. Call it magical if you want…it is art, science, math, logic and results.

You may choose to be skeptical when reading and implementing our recommendations in the book, but Feng Shui does not require your belief in order for it to work. As long as you gather the correct information about a property, you and your clients will benefit from good Feng Shui energy.

With that being said, we do find that when adjustments are made with clear intentions, while anticipating good results, we work in harmony with the universal *Law of Attraction*. This amplifies the effectiveness of Feng Shui enhancements and corrections. You will find that Chapter 10 is devoted to expanding this aspect.

In this book, you will learn the type of Feng Shui that has been practiced for thousands of years. It is a potent, compass-based method and is a more scientific approach to selecting or building a home.

Now let's take a look at some of the practical applications of Feng Shui, along with some of the corporations, people and other notables who use Feng Shui to ensure success.

While you may have an unfavorable impression of some of these people and companies, you will recognize that they have been able to amass great wealth. How they use their wealth and manage their personal and professional lives is a personal choice and not a function of Feng Shui.

The Numerous Uses of Feng Shui

Feng Shui has been used in China as a formalized and official technique for selecting auspicious sites since the Tang Dynasty. In modern times, some of the practical uses of Feng Shui are:

- Home buying and selling
- Master-planned communities
- High-rise residential structures
- Office buildings
- Apartments
- Hotels and Spas
- Remodeling homes
- Wealth-producing water features
- Investing in commercial properties
- Home evaluation and assessments
- Designing and building new homes
- New-home sales office
- Model homes for urban communities
- Identifying an ideal home
- Hospitals and physician offices
- Night clubs and restaurants
- Golf courses
- Relocating a corporate office/headquarters
- Manufacturing plants
- Development of large-scale projects
- Parks and theme parks
- Remodeling an office or corporate space
- Grocery stores
- Miniature golf courses
- Designing retaining walls
- Flipping and rehabbing properties
- Music venues and theaters
- Government buildings and offices
- Investing in rental home properties
- Designing apartment complexes
- Human-made canals, lakes and rivers
- Botanical gardens
- Kitchen and bathroom remodeling
- Airports
- Open-air concert halls
- Shopping Malls
- Retail Strip Centers
- Townhomes, condos, and patio homes

Celebrities and Major Corporations Who Use Feng Shui

Celebrities: Bob Proctor, Jack Canfield, Rhonda Burns ("The Secret Movie"), (Nielhs Bohr, Nobel Prize winner in Physics), President Donald J. Trump, Sting, Jerry Hall, Anita Roddick (Body Shop founder), Sir Richard Branson, Steven Spielberg, Deepak Chopra, Donna Karan and Tommy Hilfiger.

Corporations and High-Profile Buildings: Wall Street Journal, TELUS, Merrill Lynch, Coca-Cola, Hilton, Trump Towers, MGM Grand Hotel, Bellagio Hotel, Caesars Palace, Mirage Resorts, Casino Niagara, Cosmopolitan, Bank of America, Wells Fargo, Royal Bank of Canada, Citibank, HSBC, Texas First National, Mutual of New York, Guaranty Trust Bank of England, Chase Manhattan, Standard Charter Bank of London, Baccarat Hotel, Mandarin Oriental, Intel, White Sox Stadium, Creative Artists Agency, Aveda, American Chamber of Commerce, DreamWorks and Setai Club and Spa Wall Street.

Figure 2: The MGM Grand changed their Feng Shui to accommodate Asian guests. Previously the hotel entrance was through a lion's mouth.

There are many other corporations, celebrities and notables who use Feng Shui. However, many choose to not to disclose that publicly for a variety of reasons. While Americans love Feng Shui, they are only just beginning to learn about the classic powerful, compass-based method.

2

Identifying Good Homes to Buy, Rent, or Sell

Some properties automatically have better energy than others, primarily due to the design, setting and location.

Keep in mind that in Feng Shui *anything* extreme is taboo. Examples of this would be extreme design shaped homes, extreme drop-off on the land, extreme lot shape and so forth. In this chapter we will identify situations that will cause issues with buying or selling a home.

Please be aware that some cannot be completely corrected so price accordingly, pass on taking the listing. For most of these situations, loss of money and contractual issues are the result.

If you are buying a home, you will want to use this same information to guide you in selecting a good home to purchase.

Figure 3: Extreme designs like this home usually indicate bad health, money loss and difficult relationships.

The T-Juncture or Y-Roads Formation

A T-juncture formation is when there is a road that is directly aligned with your front door or, perhaps even the garage door. In Feng Shui, this is considered one of the most toxic formations as will cause a host of negative events for the householders. Having a good flow of energy to the front door can be good, however too much aimed at it will have the opposite effect.

This intense, direct energy is called *sha chi* or 'killing' chi. In almost all cases, it will lead to discord, money loss, divorce, accidents, and other mishaps depending on how fast and close the road is to your site. The Y-Juncture is where *two* direct roads converge at the facing of the property.

THE CURE: Block off a T-juncture with a stucco wall, a solid gate near the front door, boulders, or dense landscaping. If you are shopping for a new home, pass on these residences; even when cured they may cause issues.

Figure 4: T-juncture roads that 'aim' directly to the house produces chi/energy that is too intense. This causes **difficulties for the householders.**

Extremely Narrow-Shaped Homes

This shape for a building is known as "squeezed chi" and will not allow you to accumulate wealth. You can earn money but cannot hold onto it. Such structures can cause bankruptcy, debt and very bad health especially in the bones and joints. These configurations cut off your life blood to amass wealth—do not be tempted to take them no matter the beauty and charm they may offer.

THE CURE: Implement all the recommendations in the *To Do List* for Period 7, 8 or 9 homes (Chapters Five, Six or Seven) to further offset this feature.

Figure 5: A very narrow home design is called 'squeezed chi". It usually indicates struggles with money and getting into debt.

Homes Too Close to Highways or Fast-Moving Roads

In Feng Shui, roads and highways are considered virtual rivers and powerful purveyors of energy; this inherently can bring a certain amount of danger. The faster it moves, the further away your home should be located.

Realtors know instinctually that these properties are less desirable and will command a lower price. Modern-day highways and some busy roads are equally powerful, if not more so than rivers. When homes are too close to a highway, money will be lost because energy cannot be retained at the site.

THE CURE: Block off from view as many roads as possible with landscaping, a decorative brick wall, a courtyard or landscaping boulders. Implement all the recommendations in the *To Do List* for Period 7, 8 or 9 homes (Chapters Five, Six or Seven) to offset this feature.

Figure 6: Fast-moving roads and highways too near residential homes will negatively impact people's money and health.

Figure 7: This home has a 45° drop off into the canyon below. The home once belonged to Anna Nicole Smith.

Extreme Slopes or Sharp Drop-offs

Extreme slopes, such as a forty-five-degree incline, will cause serious money loss and a host of other very inauspicious events. A sheer cliff can be deadly; without the protection of retaining walls, your wealth will quickly slip away. If sharp drop-offs occur at the rear of the property, it can be very detrimental. People who move into or build a house on such a site will experience one bad event after another and it is almost impossible to have a harmonious and stable life.

THE CURE: Install a high retaining wall (at least 6 feet tall) anywhere on the site that has extreme slopes or drop-offs. Also implement all the recommendations in the *To Do List* for Period 7, 8 or 9 homes (Chapters Five, Six or Seven) to further offset this feature.

Water Tower, Graveyard or Electrical Tower

Homes right next to a graveyard is dead energy—people cannot thrive when you have this situation. You need vibrant, life giving energy to build wealth. Living too close to a water tower and electrical towers can also bring very bad money luck.

THE CURE: Block off the water or electrical tower with tall trees. Block off the view of the graveyard as much as possible with fencing or wall and landscaping. Also, implement all the recommendations in the *To Do List* for Period 7, 8 or 9 homes (Chapters Five, Six or Seven) to further offset this feature.

Figure 8: This water tower overwhelms the house below. This is like a mountain that is too close and becomes oppressive energy.

Storm Drains in Front of Your Home or Business

Storm drains take water away in times of flash floods, monsoons, heavy rains, and so forth. We know they serve a practical purpose. However, if you are unlucky enough to have one of these huge drains near or right in the front of your home or business, you will lose money. If the direction of this "water exit" is also bad in relation to the facing direction, it can happen very fast.

THE CURE: Block the drain from view of the front door with a short wall, a row of bushes, landscape boulders or a courtyard wall.

Figure 9: While water drains are necessary to neighborhoods, if they are located too close to the front door, it can cause money loss.

Split-level homes with three to five levels

We are not speaking of a traditional two-story home, or even a traditional three-story home, but a home with multiple levels going in all directions. A client in Salt Lake City, Utah had six levels to their home; this is extreme and will not bode well for the homeowners. It usually indicates that the family is separated, thinking is confused and in general, life is disjointed.

THE CURE: Implement all the recommendations in the *To Do List* for Period 7, 8 or 9 homes (Chapters Five, Six or Seven) to further offset this feature.

Figure 10: Split level homes can cause confusion, migraines, money loss and families breaking apart.

Homes in a Bad Location
Location, location, location!

A home that is next to or very near graveyards, police stations, excavation sites, a water tower, rail systems, electrical towers/power stations, gas station, land fill site, night club, a tall imposing building, railroad tracks, stone quarry or sewer treatment plant can create   lethargy, depression, aggressive behavior, bad health, fatal attractions, and money loss. These homes are generally offered at discounted prices. Pass on them all together; they will only cause you problems as a homeowner or investor. Real estate agents are attuned to *bad locations*.

THE CURE: Implement all the recommendations in the *To Do List* for Period 7, 8 or 9 homes (Chapters Five, Six or Seven) to further offset this feature.

Figure 11: This rail system will disrupt the energy of homes next to it and will cause negative events in the lives of the householders.

Homes Surrounded by Too Many Roads

As you know by now, roads are fast-moving purveyors of energy and they act much like a raging river. It is extremely inauspicious to be too close or have too many roads surrounding your site. Numerous roads near a home can make it vulnerable and unstable. Roads near the back of the property can be the worst. A virtual 'road' is a ditch or huge, open drains located in cities where monsoons and frequent rains can cause flooding. These sites can be so unstable they will indicate affairs, divorce, illness and all types of misfortunes.

THE CURE: Create a strong backing at the rear of the property. Insulate the site on the left and right-hand sides from the roads. Consider moving if you have experienced negative events in your life, such as money loss, disease, affairs, or sickness. Also, implement all recommendations in the *To Do List* for Period 7, 8 or 9 homes (Chapters Five, Six or Seven) to further offset this feature.

Figure 12: Several roads near or behind a house will be disruptive to the harmony of the house. Money loss is another possible outcome.

Homes on Corner Lots

When a home is located on a corner lot, this indicates certain householders may not be supported. For example, while standing in front of the home looking out, if the exposed corner is on the left-hand side then males will be affected. If the exposed corner is on the right, the females in the home may not be supported. Homes that have this land formation may sit on the market. No one seems to understand why. Now you know.

THE CURE: Add a wall, fence or row of shrubs/trees at least three feet tall on the open side if allowed by the HOA and city. Also, implement all the recommendations in the *To Do List* for Period 7, 8 or 9 homes (Chapters Five, Six or Seven) to further offset this feature.

Figure 13: This corner-lot property has a road on the right-hand side (as you're looking out) and will affect the females of the house.

Home with Side Entry

These homes affect your financial luck. It is said that money has difficulty finding its way to you. Our financial prosperity is what fuels much of our lives, so please avoid buying this type home. About this time, you may be wondering what happens to people who buy these homes and experience the negative results. There is an underlying truth about properties…your home brings you the opportunities and lessons you have chosen to experience. If you are fortunate enough to have this information before purchasing a home like this, consider yourself extremely fortunate.

THE CURE: Make the pathway to the side entrance distinct, attractive and lighted so the entrance can be easily located. Real estate agents, you may want to mention in your remarks that the entrance is on the left or right side of the house, so buyers will not be searching for it. Implement all the recommendations in the *To Do List* for Period 7, 8 or 9 homes (Chapters Five, Six or Seven) to further offset this feature.

Figure 14: This home shows an attractive walkway lighted with solar lights and a water fountain activating a prosperous flying star to help offset the side entry.

Cul-de-Sac Home

Cul-de-sac homes are tricky at best. We have observed approximately 80% of these homes are unfavorable and cause negative events for occupants. There are certain negative Feng Shui formulas that can be activated and are extremely dangerous over time. These can only be assessed by a professional audit. The circular dynamic at the end of the street tends to create chaotic energies. Additionally, the home directly aligned with the incoming street is hit by the same energy as the toxic T or Y Junction alignment. Better to pass on these settings.

THE CURE: Landscaping and wall at least 3 feet high can soften the energy coming to the house. Implement all the recommendations in the *To Do List* for Period 7, 8 or 9 homes (Chapters Five, Six or Seven) to further offset this feature.

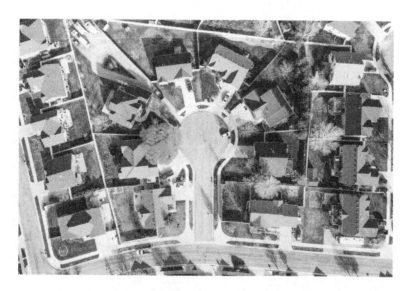

Figure 15: This cul-de-sac is short and *potentially* less harmful than homes with a longer street. A professional audit is essential to assess this accurately.

Trees, Mountains, or Poles/Columns Blocking the Front Door

The main door is extremely important because it determines how the house takes in or receives energy. Therefore, it should not be blocked by a mountain that is too close; common sense would dictate that a mountain too close or one looming over your home is just too confining. Likewise, poles or columns in direct alignment with the door or huge trees too close or too large blocking the front door is very bad Feng Shui. All of these are considered obstructions to the energy flow and can cause money issues and obstacles in your life. While trees can be removed, the other features cannot.

THE CURE: Implement all the recommendations in the *To Do List* for Period 7, 8 or 9 homes (Chapters Five, Six or Seven) to further offset this feature.

Figure 16: While there are lots of trees in the front, they do not block the door. We would still recommend editing out some of the foliage at this property.

Staircase Aligned with the Front Door

This feature blocks the flow of energy to the home. Some say it is because the stairs carry money right out the house, but the real issue is that it obstructs the energy. Staircases near the front door should be at least six (6) feet away. Buyers familiar with Feng Shui will avoid a home with this feature.

THE CURE: It is cost-prohibitive to move this feature. Implement all the recommendations in the *To Do List* for Period 7, 8 or 9 homes (Chapters Five, Six or Seven) to further offset this feature.

Figure 17: These stairs are *not* in direct alignment with the front door. While they are close, they do not block the flow of energy into the home.

Stoves on an Island

While these are extremely popular in America, it is considered bad Feng Shui to have fire in the middle of the kitchen on an island. Stoves are best placed against a wall. Buyers who are familiar with Feng Shui will avoid a home with this feature.

THE CURE: It is cost-prohibitive to move this feature. Implement all the recommendations in the *To Do List* for Period 7, 8 or 9 homes (Chapters Five, Six or Seven) to further offset this feature.

Figure 18: Stoves located on an island may cause high blood pressure or even heart attacks. Buyers familiar with Feng Shui will avoid a home with this design.

Split-level Entry

This feature is considered very negative since energy is unevenly distributed and will fall down to the lower level. While stairs are needed to an upper or lower level they should never be located near the front door.

THE CURE: It is cost-prohibitive to move this feature. Place plants to soften the confusion. Implement all the recommendations in the *To Do List* for Period 7, 8 or 9 homes (Chapters Five, Six or Seven) to further offset this feature.

Figure 19: Split-level entries are dangerous and can cause confusion. They usually indicate money loss and disharmony among the family members.

Staircase, Bathroom or Kitchen located in the Center

While this is rare, these features are considered very negative and can harm the occupants.

THE CURE: It is cost-prohibitive to move these features. Implement all the recommendations in the *To Do List* for Period 7, 8 or 9 homes (Chapters Five, Six or Seven) to further offset this feature.

Figure 20: Fire (kitchen or stove) in the middle of the house is a Feng Shui taboo. Major health issues can arise. Buyers familiar with Feng Shui will avoid this design.

Roads or Stream Directly Behind the Property

Again, we recognize roads are purveyors of energy and this is like a 'river' of energy behind the house. Depending on how large and fast (e.g. freeway or busy boulevard), it will cause money loss as well as other undesirable issues.

THE CURE: It is cost-prohibitive to move this feature. Implement all the recommendations in the *To Do List* for Period 7, 8 or 9 homes (Chapters Five, Six or Seven) to further offset this feature.

Figure 21: A stream or road located at the back of the property can indicate loss of wealth.

Water Improperly Placed

Because water is one of the most powerful elements on the planet and really the "secret" to Feng Shui, where it is placed is paramount. Please note in the *To Do List* where to place water for attracting wealth and buyers. It will also alert you where water should be turned off or relocated if possible.

THE CURE: If the improperly placed water is a large swimming pool, place large metal objects around it. Implement all the recommendations in the *To Do List* for Period 7, 8 or 9 homes (Chapters Five, Six or Seven)) to further offset this feature.

Figure 22: This pool is located too close to the home and in Feng Shui is referred to as 'cutting feet". It generally indicates money loss.

Bathroom over the Front Door, Kitchen, or Bedroom

In Feng Shui bathrooms are considered 'unclean' and therefore should not be located over where you enter the home, sleep or eat.

THE CURE: It is cost-prohibitive to move these features. Implement all the recommendations in the *To Do List* for Period 7, 8 or 9 homes (Chapters Five, Six or Seven) Chapters Four, Five or Six) to further offset this feature.

Figure 23: Toilets should not be located over the front door, kitchen or a bedroom.

Bathroom/Toilets Near or Facing the Front Door

The energy of a bathroom or toilet should not be located near or facing the front door. It will diminish the good energy located there.

THE CURE: Keep the door closed especially during showings. Keep the toilet lids down on all toilets (except when in use) and be sure toilets are photographed with the seat lids down. It is cost-prohibitive to move this feature. Implement all the recommendations in the *To Do List* for Period 7, 8 or 9 homes (Chapters Five, Six or Seven) to further offset this feature.

Figure 24: Guest bathrooms should not be located too near the front door. If wealth energy is located there, it will diminish it.

Sharp, Circular Driveways and Diving Driveways

These designs are considered negative energy and can ignite a host of undesirable events for the occupants. Driveways that 'dive' to the front door are common in mountainous or hilly areas of the world.

THE CURE: It is cost-prohibitive to move this feature. Implement all the recommendations in the *To Do List* for Period 7, 8 or 9 homes (Chapters Four, Five or Six) to further offset this feature.

Figure 25: Circular driveways can be fine if they are not extreme. In this photo the driveway has a soft pass by to the front door and is good.

Exposed Beams

Decorative ceiling beams that are eight (8) feet or lower are harmful to the occupants. Sleeping under these beams can cause couples to divorce and lots of health issues. High coffered ceilings are not a problem.

THE CURE: It is cost-prohibitive to move this feature. Implement all the recommendations in the *To Do List* for Period 7, 8 or 9 homes (Chapters Five, Six or Seven) to further offset this feature.

Figure 26: Overhead beams located too near the body can cause a host of health issues.

Death and Empty Lines or Void Lines

There are specific door degrees that can bring bad luck to a property. The door degree means the exact compass direction that it faces. They call these disaster degrees Kong Wang or Kun Mang: *Death and Empty Lines* (DEL) or Void Lines. The most serious DELs are the exact cardinal points; 90° (East), 180° (South), 270° (West), and 360°/0° (North). Since DELs open a "window" in which energy, ghosts, or spirits can enter, they are best reserved for sacred spaces like churches, otherwise spirits or discarnate energy could enter, via these specific degrees, into a building. This is also why some properties do not sell and may languish on the market. Homes located next to graveyards, churches, or that have landscaping and trees blocking the light may shift into a DEL.

THE CURE: Take a DEL-oriented door off its hinges for about an hour and then re-hang it. Homes will settle over time and ease into these unlucky degrees if you are surrounded by a yin (dark, quiet, dead) environment. Doors will go into a DEL if a structure has been closed or empty for a while.

Figure 27: When empty homes sit on the market for long periods of time, the doors can move into a DEL. This is because the energy becomes 'dead chi'. See how to clear this energy in Chapter 7.

3

How to Quickly Sell a Property

Before we start implementing the changes for your home or listing, let's address the 'good,' the 'bad' and the 'ugly.'

There will be things you will not be able to change such as the location, home design, pool location, etc. If those items are industry agreed turn-offs, price the property accordingly. Now we will determine the 'good' aspects to focus on.

THE GOOD

Signage

Appealing professional signage that is in pristine condition is a must. Your signage should represent the general market for that price home. Million-dollar+ listings require luxury signage. Signs for median price homes need to reflect standards for those neighborhoods. You will also want to check with the homeowner's association (HOA) for specific signage and post requirements for each community. Make certain you are complying with their rules. Good relations with the HOA can help you sell a property.

Figure 28: A good sign in pristine condition is essential for attracting buyers.

The Sales Price

For Feng Shui purposes, use good numbers to price the home and to make counter offers. The good numbers are 1, 4, 6, 8 and 9. Avoid the 2, 3, 5 and 7. However, if you work with Asian buyers, it is best to avoid the number 4. It holds a negative connotation to them because in the Chinese language the number *four* sounds similar to the word *death.*

The number 8 or *ba* is considered the luckiest in the Chinese culture because its pronunciation is similar to *fa*, which means wealth, fortune and prosperity in the Chinese language. Favorable numbers are highly regarded in many cultures. Research indicates that it can be very beneficial, especially when working with particular clients.

Realtor.com posted an article in 2016 entitled *The Lucky Numbers That Can Drive Up Your Home's Value*. According to their research, there were 178 homes on realtor.com priced at either $888,888 or $8,888,888. Those homes were concentrated mainly in areas with large Asian populations. You must admit, it is an eye-catching strategy. Here's how you can use it. If your listing is priced at $350,000, make a simple adjustment and list it at $349,999 or going up in price, change it to $368,900.

Marketing
Have great professional photos and a video taken of the property after it has been is cleaned, cleared and properly staged. It is ideal to have twilight, daylight drone photos and a video, especially for luxury properties. This is a place you want to invest so you get the best possible results. Even median priced homes deserve this kind of attention to detail for your clients.

These photos are most often the buyer's first introduction to a property. You truly won't get a second chance to make a good first impression. These images will span the internet and become *your* calling card. Be proud of what you put into that vast space. Understand that you now have a global presence and outreach.

Take time to carefully review the photos. Then write appropriate remarks for the detailed MLS listing report as well as all other related marketing and advertising copy. Imagine yourself as the buyer who is looking for that exact home. How would you describe the home so they can envision themselves visiting the property, falling in love with it, tendering an offer, closing escrow and moving into that home? WOW…what a feeling to help make dreams come true! Take time to translate those feelings and vision into words. If that isn't your strong suit, find someone who can do this for you. It is that important!

Homes priced at $888,888 or $8,888,888 as well as addresses with multiple 8's are popular in many communities

The Front Door

This area is an essential focal point. It is where buyers enter and again, the first impression of their initial visit is crucial. Make it stand out in the most appealing manner. This includes the condition of the entry door, doorframe and door hardware. These need to be in excellent condition with the door easy to open and close.

Figure 29: This front door has a charming arch and has a winding path leading to it.

If the home has a confusing entrance such as side door that is difficult to locate, find a way to direct potential buyers. This can be done with a beautiful sidewalk, or a lovely sign. Properly placed water features that greet you at the front entrance should be pristine. Potted plants or flowers should be vibrant and free of dead foliage. A welcome mat is nice but be selective in the wording if it has any. Elegant is better than cute or funny.

Stage to Sell

Expectations are very high for the modern-day home buyer. Television shows such as *HGTV* (Home & Garden TV) are largely responsible for this and have captured the public's imagination with their compelling programs. Their most popular series cover topics on decorating, remodeling, staging, flipping, and restoration, all for the purpose of increasing buyer appeal and property value.

You may already have talents to accomplish this. If not, hire a professional stager to get the home looking its very best. If appropriate, an interior designer may be brought in if the home needs some slight remodeling. This can yield remarkable results.

We have all walked into homes where there are dozens of artifacts of all kinds and from every culture. You immediately know, that in its current state, this is only going to appeal to a one in a million buyer. Since selling is the objective, it is imperative to create a neutral pallet so that as many buyers as possible can envision living comfortably in the home.

Professional stagers and designers have a way of communicating with sellers and explaining the benefits of packing and storing their personal collections. Sellers learn that when this depersonalization occurs buyers can picture themselves living in the home. The bonus effect is that the sellers are now free to imagine themselves in a new space. A staging professional can be just the buffer you need to convince sellers that this necessary step is in their best interest.

Curb Appeal

This property characteristic goes hand-in-hand with the importance of the entry door. Buyers' typical assessment of a property is through the curb appeal they see in online photos. Make sure that their initial reaction is favorable. Allow the beauty on the outside, to invite them inside for an interior inspection.

Whatever the style of the exterior of a property, make certain it is well-maintained. This includes all types of landscaping. Whether the property is English garden style, Oriental, formal, informal, woodland, xeriscape or desert landscaping, make sure it shows that both the front and backyards are well-tended.

THE BAD

Figure 30: This home has great curb appeal. The charm of this house would invite potential buyers to take a look inside.

Animals and House Pets

Almost everyone loves pets. However, there are some people who are allergic, frightened or simply do not care to be around pets. It is not personal, it is just a fact. There are some pets that react unfavorably to certain people and situations. Home showings can be very stressful to all pets.

It is best for animals to be removed from the house during showings if at all possible. Another alternative is kenneling pets if no one is available to take them out of the house during showings. This is not ideal for several reasons and if they are not accustomed to being kenneled, it can be very traumatic.

Odors in the House

Have you ever been in a house when someone was cooking a delicious fish dinner? While the meal is being cooked, we seem to adjust to the fishy smell in anticipation of a fabulous feast. However, someone who may walk in afterwards could be repelled by the lingering fish smell.

There are all sorts of repugnant odors such as pets, smoke, fish, spices, cooking and even strong chemical deodorizers. Some can be easily treated by removing the source; others require deeper methods of wall washing, carpet removal, repainting, vent cleaning, and so forth. Odors can negatively impact the sale of an otherwise lovely home. This type of feedback is very common from home buyers and needs to be addressed. Keep a vendor list handy for your clients if this is an issue.

THE UGLY

Clutter

Clutter of any kind, seen or unseen, creates negative energy and needs to be removed or organized. As the depersonalization of a listing is occurring, this is the perfect time to eliminate clutter. This means in those hidden spaces as well. Potential buyers will open closets, drawers, attics and so forth.

Barbara had a client who was experiencing a lot of chaos in her life and was ready to find a solution. During the consultation, Barbara did not notice any *obvious* clutter. Then the client opened a kitchen drawer to locate her checkbook. The contents popped out like a jack-in-the-box!

After this explosion, Barbara asked if that was the designated 'junk drawer'. The client said, "No, all my drawers are like this." She then opened all drawers throughout the house and voila! Here was the underlying clutter and chaos! The next step was a hiring a professional organizer. Afterward, the client reported peace and harmony returned to her home and life.

Backyards

Unkempt yards or those that are void of plants will repel buyers even if the house has been remodeled and ready to sell after a great update. This is an essential aspect of great curb appeal and one that requires either time or attention by the homeowner or a professional landscaping remedy. Either way, it is an investment that pays dividends toward the sale of a property.

4

Feng Shui Toolbox

These tools will help you stay on task and keep your clients actively engaged while implementing adjustments.

Recap

Let's review what you have learned so far:

- Feng Shui is a phenomenon that has captured the attention of successful corporations and very wealthy people globally. Now it is your turn to tap into those same resources.

- You hold in your hands the Feng Shui formulas and energetic methods that you can use to your and your clients' advantage. Get proficient and comfortable with them.

- You have examined how to identify good homes to Buy, Rent or Sell and the issues to avoid. Remember those.

- The Good, Bad and Ugly indicate where to focus your energy. Apply that knowledge to create optimal results.

Keep in mind that the Feng Shui and energetic adjustments provided in this book are aimed at expediting the sale of a property. We have also identified the most important things to look for when purchasing a home.

Please note that if you are buying or living in a home, there are additional Feng Shui formulas that are important to consider. For example, the stove's location and direction affect virtually every aspect of life (wealth, health and relationships). However, those are not in the scope of this book. There are techniques that are briefly discussed in the *Bonus Chapter* of this book that will provide a glimpse into the depth and additional uses of Feng Shui.

With that being said, implementing the correct *To Do List* in either Chapter 5, 6 or 7 while incorporating the information in Chapters 8, 9, 10, and 11 will provide the quick sales results you want to achieve when properly activated. Before starting the actual Step-by-Step process, we are going to provide you some important guidelines.

Doing Things with Intention and Taking Inspired Action
At first, the steps you take may feel unfamiliar. Set aside any judgment you may have and keep your mind open to all the good possibilities you are allowing for you and your client.

During and after applying the adjustments, you may be "nudged" or have a "hunch" to take a particular action. It may be reaching out to someone (maybe a previous client), visiting a specific Open House or coffee shop, calling a friend, rewriting the MLS listing remarks or any number of things that are inspired by an "ah-ha" moment. These inspired thoughts may seem random, but when acted upon they usually lead to wonderful synchronicities. Take your time, slow down a bit, ask questions, listen and respond to these important messages.

Look at each adjustment as a job assignment you are giving to the particular object you are placing or action you are taking. Learn to be comfortable talking to homes and objects similar to the way you talk to animals and small children. If you are not familiar with this concept, then think of something or someone you hold dear and remember how you talk to them when you want them to assist you with a project. Be kind, loving, thoughtful and grateful. You are eliciting their help.

Figure 31: Requesting helpful assistance...see, you know how to do this!

Yes, inanimate objects receive and respond to our thoughts, feelings and mental imagery. Everything is energy…remember? They love to collaborate with us. You have more assistance than you ever imagined, don't you? Everything is conspiring in your favor! If anyone asks who you are talking to, tell them you are having a staff meeting. On the other hand, you may simply want to have these conversations in the privacy of your mind.

Even if you do not fully understand how this works, trust the process and leave yourself open to expanding your ability to communicate with everything. We KNOW you are a great communicator, or you would not be in this industry!

How to Place Cures and Activate Enhancements

You are not quite ready to place cures or activate enhancements yet, but you need to know the process so you feel more prepared to begin your *Step-by-Step Feng Shui Guide* and the appropriate *Checklists*. For now, just absorb this information and keep it tucked away for when you start curing and enhancing the energies.

Important Note!

Always choose to place the recommended Feng Shui cures first to *neutralize the negative energy* in the areas indicated in the appropriate *To Do List*. You will learn more about choosing the correct *To Do List* in the following pages.

When you are placing the Cures, you will announce your intention to the object you are activating while you are placing it. For example, "You are curing the negative energy in the Southeast (or whatever direction is affected) of this property. Thank you for doing a great job of neutralizing the negative energies here so we attract the right buyers for this property."

After all the Cures have been placed, you will activate the enhancements noted on the *To Do List* for that specific property. The same process occurs for placing enhancements. Except, you announce to the area and object, "You are *enhancing* the positive energy in the Southwest (or whatever direction you are addressing) of this property. Thank you for doing such an amazing job of multiplying the good energies here so we attract the right buyers for this property."

Getting Organized to Implement Adjustments
In the following pages you will find your "FENG SHUI TOOLBOX" which provides the essential tools you will need for each property.

1. Seller's Feng Shui Checklist – Page 62
2. Buyer's Feng Shui Checklist – Page 63
3. Property Checklist – Page 64
4. Step-by-Step Feng Shui Guide – Page 65
5. How to Determine the Facing Directions – Page 66
6. How to Take a Compass Direction Reading with Smartphone GPS App – Page 67
7. Compass Direction Chart – Page 68
8. How to Divide Floor Plans – Page 69
9. The Cardinal Directions – Page 70
10. The Intercardinal Directions – Page 71
11. Cures and Enhancements Examples/Tips – Pages 72-77
12. Ba Qua to Sell a House Faster – Pages 78-79

You will want to make a copy of either *the Buyer's or Seller's Feng Shui Checklist*, the P*roperty Checklist* and *the Step-by-Step Feng Shui Guide* to use with each property floorplan. You will use these to make notes specific to each home that will guide you to implement the appropriate adjustments.

Yes, you will need a floorplan of the property. It can be a hand-drawn sketch that is close to scale or a professional blueprint.

When we work from a blueprint, we go to a printing service and have it reduced to an easily handled size. Keep a "master copy" in case you need to make additional copies.

Follow the directions for each of the tools you will be using and you will find yourself confident using this process quickly.

It is a great idea for you to practice this on your own home before doing this for your clients. Of course, you will not want to activate the "sales techniques" for your own property during your practice session. If you do that, you may find someone showing up at your door to purchase your property. You **can** cure and enhance the energies noted on your *To Do List* with the intention of fully supporting you and your family. Now we will view the contents of your new Feng Shui Toolbox.

Figure 32: The following pages provide your professional Feng Shui Tools to create the desired results; keep them close by for easy access.

Seller's Feng Shui Checklist	
✓	**ACTION ITEMS**
	Assess property using your new Feng Shui eyes ~ Use the PROPERTY *CHECKLIST* here ~ (Page 64)
	Implement Feng Shui recommendations using: • Correct Period (7, 8 or 9) • Correct facing direction of N, NE, E, SE, S, SW, W, NW plus whether it is the Exact Direction of 1, 2 or 3 See Compass Direction Chart on Page 68
	Provide sellers a personalized guide for releasing their home and imagining the next phase of their life in a new location – See Chapter 9 for examples.
	Stage the home for new owners to envision themselves living there – depersonalize and keep it show ready
	Professional photos and video
	Professional signage
	Personalized marketing to the neighborhood
	Online marketing, including unique Social Media video
	Celebratory Open House (if owners agree)
	Provide concise showing instructions without lots of limitations and respond quickly to showing requests
	Respond to all offers in a prompt, friendly, professional manner
	Negotiate professionally
	When under contract, keep your clients and the other agent informed during the transaction. Send a letter to your clients noting the important contract dates and detailed information about how the transaction will progress.
	Home inspections are handled differently in various locations, so prepare the owner with specifics (have utilities on, leave the property during inspection, etc.)
	Closing Day – make advance appointment with closing agent or mobile notary, attend closing, take congratulatory photo and post online if permitted

Buyers' Feng Shui Checklist	
✓	**ACTION ITEMS**
	Assess property using your new Feng Shui eyes ~ Use the *PROPERTY CHECKLIST* here ~ (Page 64)
	Provide buyers a personalized guide for releasing their current home and imagining their new home – See Chapter 9 for examples
	Have the buyers provide a list of their "must haves" and "bonus amenities" – realize that these may shift over time and be willing to adjust accordingly
	Have fun with the process and make it a collaborative adventure with your clients. The higher vibe you maintain, the faster the manifestation
	Keep water and healthy snacks in a cooler in your car to keep everyone hydrated and energized
	Show no more than 3-4 homes in a day and keep notes of your clients' comments. If you preview homes before showing and use your *Feng Shui Buyers Checklist*, you can eliminate a lot of unnecessary showings
	Make offer based on comparable analysis of like properties
	Put a personal message from the buyers to the sellers as to why they want to purchase the house. This can make a difference in multiple offer situations
	Negotiate professionally and respond promptly
	When under contract, keep your clients and the other agent informed during the transaction. Send letter to your clients noting the important contract dates and detailed information about how the transaction will progress
	Closing day – make advance appointment with closing agent or mobile notary, attend closing, take congratulatory photo and post online if permitted

PROPERTY CHECKLIST
(USE YOUR STEP-BY-STEP FENG SHUI GUIDE – PAGE 66)

CLIENT CONTACT INFORMATION		
Name:		
Address:		
Phone:		
Email:		
HOUSE/PROPERTY INFORMATION	**Page**	**Data**
Move-in or Remodel Date = *Period* 7, 8 or 9	65	
Home facing or front door compass degree	66-69	
Interior garage door compass degree	67-68	
Back door compass degree	67-68	
LANDFORMS & DESIGN (Yes or No)	**Page**	**Y/N**
T-Juncture or Y-Roads	24	
Extremely narrow-shaped homes	25	
Home too close to highways or fast roads	26	
Extreme slopes or drop-offs	27	
Water tower, graveyard or electrical tower	28	
Storm drains in front of home or business	29	
Split-level homes with 3 or more levels	30	
Home in bad location	31	
Home surrounded by too many roads	32	
Home on corner lot	33	
Home with Side Entry	34	
Cul de Sac	35	
Trees, mountains or poles blocking front door	36	
Staircase aligned with front door	37	
Stove on an island	38	
Split-level entry	39	
Staircase, bathroom or kitchen in center	40	
Road or stream directly behind the property	41	
Water improperly placed (*see Chapters 4,5 & 6*)	42	
Bathroom over front door, kitchen or bedroom	43	
Bathroom/toilet near or facing front door	44	
Sharp, circular and diving driveway	45	
Exposed Beams	46	
DEL - Death & Empty Lines or void line	47	
Use Ba Gua to Sell the House Faster	78-79	
Suggestions from Chapters 8, 9, 10 & 11	137-178	

Step-by-Step Feng Shui Guide

Step 1: Get the Move-In Date

To implement the Feng Shui correctly, you will need the 'Time Period' in which you or your clients moved into the home. If the moved-in date was Period 7 and major renovations were done in Period 8, the house is now a Period 8 home. In this case, you would refer to the recommendations in Chapter 6 - Period 8.

Period 7: Moved-in between Feb 4, 1984 to Feb 3, 2004
Period 8: Moved-in between Feb 4, 2004 to Feb 3, 2024
Period 9: Moved-in between Feb 4, 2024 to Feb 3, 2044

Step 2: Take a Compass Direction

Once you have determined the facing direction (page 66), put your back to the house front, facing the street and use your smartphone compass app (page 67). It will give you a digital read out like 92° East for example. Refer to the *Compass Direction Chart* on page 68 to determine the Feng Shui directional term. For example, 92° is referred to as East 2. **IMPORTANT: Only use the app for exact numerical degrees such as 92°.**

Step 3: Divide the Floor Plan

You will need a simple floor plan and divide it up like a tic-tac-toe grid into 9 equal sections as shown on page 69. Professionally drafted floorplans are preferable when available.

Step 4: Indicate the Eight Directions

Overlay the eight directions (the center is the 9th section). The Cardinal directions are North, South, East and West. The Intercardinal directions are Southeast, Southwest, Northwest and Northeast. Refer to page 70 and 71. This will show you where to write the directions on the floor plan.

Step 5: Implement the Accurate *To Do List*

Once you have the correct facing direction and time Period for the property, go to that section and start putting the recommendations into action. Based on the Period and compass direction, you will refer to either Chapter 5, 6 or 7.

Step 6: Space Clearing

If you feel the house has negative or stagnate energy, you may want to do a space clearing. Refer to Chapter 8 for more details on this process.

Step 7: Install the Ba Gua Image

To speed up the sale of the home, place the Ba Gua under the front door rug. It can be placed inside, outside or both. See pages 78 and 79.

Step 8: Law of Attraction, Affirmations & Clear Intentions

Go to Chapters 8 through 11 for more details on these amazing methods to overcome obstacles and attract more of what you want to achieve.

How to Determine the Facing Directions

House #1 shown below is how most homes are built; the front door faces the street. Take the compass direction at the door. In house #2 and #3, these front doors cannot be used as the 'facing' direction. Stand in the center of the front yard facing the street and take the compass reading from there.

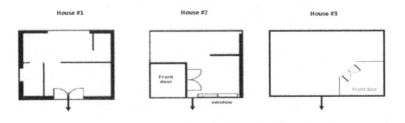

Figure 33: This house has a side 'front' door. Take the compass direction by standing in the center of the front yard, facing the street. While the front door is important, it cannot be used to find the correct 'energy chart' for a house.

How to Take a Compass Direction Reading with Smartphone GPS App

If the **front door** faces the street, put your back to the door and take a reading. See Barbara below taking a compass direction with her smartphone. If the front door does not face the street, stand in the center of the front yard and face the street and take the reading. Stand still, otherwise the GPS will keep changing the degree.

The following image is from an Android. You will see a digital read out like the photo below. Once you have the exact degree, refer to the *Direction Chart* on the next page to get the exact direction in Feng Shui terms. For example, on the Android it says 136° SE. Referring to the *Direction Chart*, this is Southeast 2 in Feng Shui terms. This is important since the adjustments for Southeast 1 are different from Southeast 2 on the *To Do List*. You may also use a traditional hiking compass by following the manufacturer's directions. Feng Shui masters and practitioners use a Luo Pan (see the image on page 183).

Important Note: Some apps do not register the correct compass direction, so ALWAYS use the numerical degrees for accuracy.

Compass Direction Chart

General Direction	Exact Direction	Compass Degrees
SOUTH	South 1	157.6° - 172.5°
	South 2	172.6° - 187.5°
	South 3	187.6° - 202.5°
SOUTHWEST	Southwest 1	202.6° - 217.5°
	Southwest 2	217.6° - 232.5°
	Southwest 3	232.6° - 247.5°
WEST	West 1	247.6° - 262.5°
	West 2	262.6° - 277.5°
	West 3	277.6° - 292.5°
NORTHWEST	Northwest 1	292.6° - 307.5°
	Northwest 2	307.6° - 322.5°
	Northwest 3	322.6° - 337.5°
NORTH	North 1	337.6° - 352.5°
	North 2	352.6° - 7.5°
	North 3	7.6° - 22.5°
NORTHEAST	Northeast 1	22.6° - 37.5°
	Northeast 2	37.6° - 52.5°
	Northeast 3	52.6° - 67.5°
EAST	East 1	67.6° - 82.5°
	East 2	82.6° - 97.5°
	East 3	97.6° - 112.5°
SOUTHEAST	Southeast 1	112.6° - 127.5°
	Southeast 2	127.6° - 142.5°
	Southeast 3	142.6° - 157.5°

How to Divide Floor Plans

Divide the floor plan in 9 even sections like tic-tac-toe. Overlay the correct compass directions. Refer to the charts on pages 70 and 71 to see where the directions will be allocated per your house facing. You will need this information to place water, cures, furniture and so forth. Remember each room also has all eight directions plus the center. *It is a microcosm of the macrocosm.*

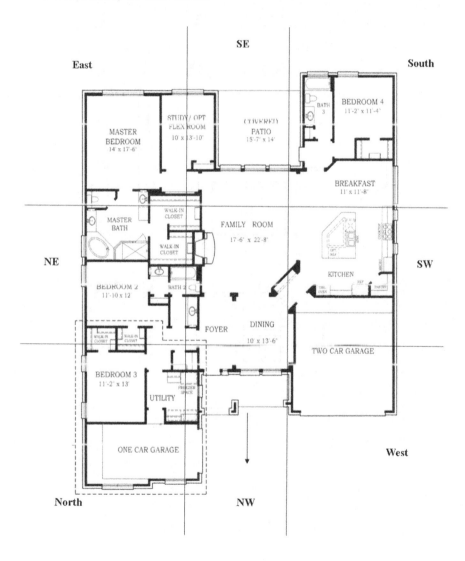

The Cardinal Directions

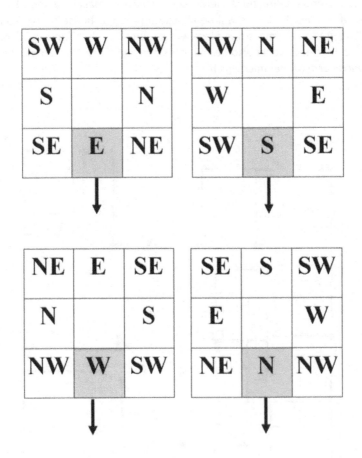

The Intercardinal Directions

W	NW	N
SW		NE
S	SE	E

↓

N	NE	E
NW		SE
W	SW	S

↓

E	SE	S
NE		SW
N	NW	W

↓

S	SW	W
SE		NW
E	NE	N

↓

Cures and Enhancements Examples

The following recommendations on the *To Do Lists* in Chapters 5, 6 or 7 to extract the best energy whether you intend to sell or not. The recommendations are based on the powerful *Flying Stars* system because it yields quick results. **Note that it is important to do the cures first, then the enhancements.** Here are some examples of the cures and enhancements you will use to change and balance the energy of homes:

Water is generally used as an enhancement for wealth. This can be fountains, pools, ponds, spas, hot tubs, waterfalls and so forth. Be sure that your water enrichment is proportional to the size of the home. A small fountain holding two gallons of water will not be sufficient for a 4,000 square foot house. We will also alert you where water should *not* be placed as it may cause money loss, disease or contractual issues/lawsuits.

Figure 34: Water is used to enhance wealth and prosperity in Feng Shui.

Mountains (Earth) in Feng Shui are represented by landscape mounds, courtyard walls, boulders, stone/concrete statues, heavy planters or pots. If you have a real mountain in the recommended area, you are indeed blessed! Courtyard walls are a good cure for blocking off a T-Juncture road coming directly to the house. If installing some of the larger 'mountains' such as boulders is not possible, make use of tall (3 feet or more) heavy earthen pots or planters.

Figure 35: Anything 3 feet and higher is considered a 'mountain' in Feng Shui. Real earth materials work best such as stone, granite, boulders or even a landscape mound as seen on golf courses.

Metal is used as an effective cure for negative energy. The best is high-quality metals such as bronze, brass, copper, stainless steel and pewter. It can be metal statues, metal art, metal kick plate on a door or wind chimes. Aluminum outdoor furniture or wrought iron is not a sufficient cure. Wind chimes, while often made of aluminum, are considered a good cure because they move and have sound. When metal wind chimes are used as a cure, they should be at least 3 feet in length.

Figure 36: Metal is used to cure or enhance energy.

Fire is used to either cure or enhance energy. Real fire is best such as a fireplace, fire pit or torches or very large candles or group of candles. If a real fire feature cannot be used then make use of fire colors (red, fuchsia, purple, or orange). Red-colored paint or textiles such as drapes or rugs can also be used in the recommended area.

Figure 37: Fire is used to enhance or cure negative energy.

Swimming Pools

If a swimming pool is badly placed, it can cause a host of negative events including money loss and contractual issues. If we recommend that you cure this area, you will need big metal. Here are some ideas of the amount to cure this big water!

Figure 38: If a pool is badly placed it will need big metal placed near-by to cure it.

Common Sense Tips

- Place Cures FIRST, then place enhancements
- Set your intentions with each placement as noted below (out loud or silently)
  - "This is <u>curing</u> the negative energy in the "DIRECTION" (N, S, E, W, NE, NW, SE, SW)
  - "This is <u>enhancing</u> the good energy in the "DIRECTION" (N, S, E, W, NE, NW, SE, SW)
- When placing cures and enhancements make sure they are aesthetically pleasing from a design perspective
- Some cures noted on the *To Do Lists* are obvious outside cures, such as birdbaths and wind chimes
- When a pool needs to be cured it is important to place the cures near the pool
- Learn to use ALL the tools in your Feng Shui Toolbox proficiently

Figure 39: Use all your professional abilities including your newly acquired Feng Shui Toolbox skills.

Ba Gua to Sell a House Faster

Place under the front doormat or rug (inside or outside or *both*); turn the image to face OUT to the correct home facing. For example, a North facing home will have the North facing trigram toward the street.

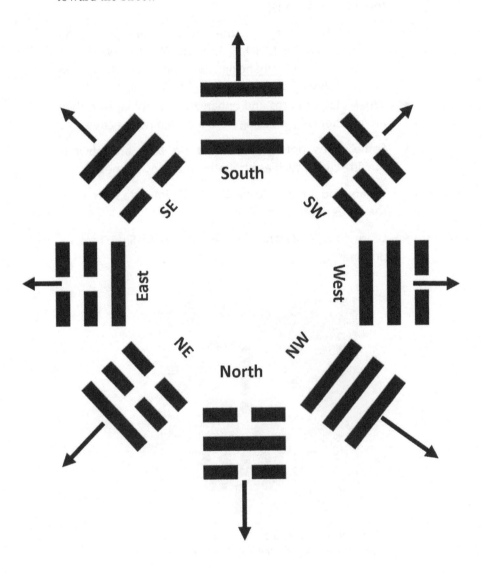

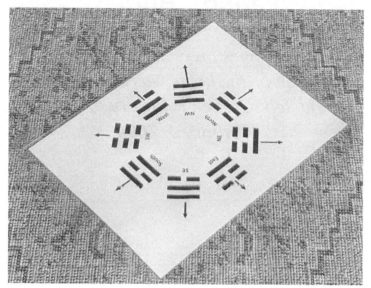

Figure 40: Place the Ba Gua under a doormat. Turn it to the home's facing direction. In our example here, the Ba Gua is turned out to face Southeast.

5

Fast Sell: Step-by-Step for Period 7 Homes

*Period 7 homes are when the occupants moved in or the home was substantially remodeled between **February 4, 1984 to February 3, 2004**.*

This 'period' of time is essential in order to implement the correct Feng Shui for the property. Before you start the *To Do List* recommendations, you will need to do the following:

- Make certain you have the correct move-in date *(Period 7)* if you are in this section of the book.
- Take a compass direction of the property
- Divide the floor plan into 9 sections (tic-tac-toe)
- Write the directions on the outside of floor plan
- Note the *To Do List* adjustments on the floor plan to implement easily

Refer to page 67 to see how to take a compass direction. See page 69 to see how to divide up the floor plan. Refer to pages 70-71 to see where to place the eight directions after locating the facing direction. See the *example on the next page* and implement the recommended adjustments.

NOTE: Place cures first, then the enhancements.

Figure 41: Stand in the front of the house facing the street to take the compass direction.

Example: **Period 7, North 1** house. Install water fountain in front, place birdbath or red rug in the South, and hang wind chimes in the West. Beds placed on North or East walls will enjoy the best energy. See the **North 1** *To Do List* for other recommendations.

To Do List

SOUTH 1 Homes that face **157.6° to 172.5°**
PERIOD 7 (Moved-in Feb 4, 1984 to Feb 3, 2004)

NW	N	SE
W		E
SW	S	SE

Water	*Cure or Remove/Turn Off:* WATER in the SW and SE *Enhancement:* WATER in the NE or NW *e.g. water fountain, pool, pond, spa, hot tub, or waterfall*
Mountain	*Enhancement:* MOUNTAIN in the North *e.g. boulders, landscape mounds, walls, stone statue or sculpture at least 3 feet tall*
Metal	*Cure:* METAL in the SW and SE *e.g. metal 6-hollow rod wind chimes, door kick plate, planter, pot, statue or sculpture*
Fire	*Cure:* FIRE in the South *e.g. firepit, fireplace, torches, group of candles, red colored rug or paint South-facing doors red*
Directions	*Enhancement:* Use doors facing NW, North, NE, and West for prosperity *e.g. use these doors frequently*

To Do List

NW	N	SE
W		E
SW	S	SE

SOUTH 2 and 3 Homes that face **172.6° to 202.5°**
PERIOD 7 (Moved-in Feb 4, 1984 to Feb 3, 2004)

Water	*Cure or Remove/Turn Off:* WATER in NE and NW *Enhancement:* WATER in SW or SE *e.g. water fountain, pool, pond, spa, hot tub, or waterfall*
Mountain	*Enhancement:* MOUNTAIN in the South *e.g. boulders, landscape mounds, walls, stone statue or sculpture at least 3 feet tall*
Metal	*Cure:* METAL in the NE and NW *e.g. metal 6-hollow rod wind chimes, door kick plate, planter, pot, statue or sculpture*
Fire	*Cure:* FIRE in the North *e.g. firepit, fireplace, torches, group of candles, red colored rug or paint North-facing doors red*
Directions	*Enhancement:* Use doors facing West, SW, South, SE and East for prosperity *e.g. use these doors frequently*

To Do List

N	NE	E
NW		SE
W	**SW**	S

SW 1 Homes that face **202.6° to 217.5°**
PERIOD 7 (Moved-in Feb 4, 1984 to Feb 3, 2004)

Water	*Cure or Remove/Turn Off:* WATER in the SE, West and NW *Enhancement:* WATER in the North or NE *e.g. water fountain, pool, pond, spa, hot tub, or waterfall*
Mountain	*Enhancement:* MOUNTAIN in the East *e.g. boulders, landscape mounds, walls, stone statue or sculpture at least 3 feet tall*
Metal	*Cure:* METAL in the SE, West and NW *e.g. metal 6-hollow rod wind chimes, door kick plate, planter, pot, statue or sculpture*
Fire	*Cure:* FIRE in the SW *e.g. firepit, fireplace, torches, group of candles, red colored rug or paint Southwest-facing doors red*
Directions	*Enhancement:* Use doors facing North, NE, East and South for prosperity *e.g. use these doors frequently*

To Do List

N	NE	E
NW		SE
W	SW	S

SW 2 and 3 Homes that face **217.6° to 247.5°**
PERIOD 7 (Moved-in Feb 4, 1984 to Feb 3, 2004)

Water	*Cure or Remove/Turn Off:* WATER in the NW, East and SE
	Enhancement: WATER in the South or SW *e.g. water fountain, pool, pond, spa, hot tub, or waterfall*
Mountain	*Enhancement:* MOUNTAIN in the West *e.g. boulders, landscape mounds, walls, stone statue or sculpture at least 3 feet tall*
Metal	*Cure:* METAL in the NW and East *e.g. metal 6-hollow rod wind chimes, door kick plate, planter, pot, statue or sculpture*
Fire	*Cure:* FIRE in the NE *e.g. firepit, fireplace, torches, group of candles, red colored rug or paint Northeast-facing doors red*
Directions	*Enhancement:* Use doors facing North, South, SW, and West for prosperity *e.g. use these doors frequently*

To Do List

NE	E	SE
N		S
NW	**W**	SW

WEST 1 Homes that face **247.6° to 262.5°**
PERIOD 7 (Moved-in Feb 4, 1984 to Feb 3, 2004)

Water	*Cure or Remove/Turn Off:* Water in the North, West and NE *Enhancement:* WATER in the SE or NW *e.g. water fountain, pool, pond, spa, hot tub, or waterfall*
Mountain	*Enhancement:* MOUNTAIN in the NE *e.g. boulders, landscape mounds, walls, stone statue or sculpture at least 3 feet tall*
Metal	*Cure:* METAL in the North and West *e.g. metal 6-hollow rod wind chimes, door kick plate, planter, pot, statue or sculpture*
Fire	*Cure:* FIRE in the East and NE *e.g. firepit, fireplace, torches, group of candles, red colored rug or paint doors that face East or Northeast red*
Directions	*Enhancement:* Use doors facing SE, South, SW and NW for prosperity *e.g. use these doors frequently*

To Do List

NE	E	SE
N		S
NW	W	SW

WEST 2 and 3 Homes that face **262.6° to 292.5°**
PERIOD 7 (Moved-in Feb 4, 1984 to Feb 3, 2004)

Water	*Cure or Remove/Turn Off:* WATER in the South, East and SW *Enhancement:* WATER in the NW or SE *e.g. water fountain, pool, pond, spa, hot tub, or waterfall*
Mountain	*Enhancement:* MOUNTAIN in the SW *e.g. boulders, landscape mounds, walls, stone statue or sculpture at least 3 feet tall*
Metal	*Cure:* METAL in the East and South *e.g. metal 6-hollow rod wind chimes, door kick plate, planter, pot, statue or sculpture*
Fire	*Cure:* FIRE in the West and SW *e.g. firepit, fireplace, torches, group of candles, red colored rug or paint doors that face West or Southwest red*
Directions	*Enhancement:* Use doors facing SE, NW, North and NE for prosperity *e.g. use these doors frequently*

To Do List

NW1 Homes that face **292.6° to 307.5°**
PERIOD 7 (Moved-in Feb 4, 1984 to Feb 3, 2004)

E	SE	S
NE		SW
N	NW	W

Water	*Cure or Remove/Turn Off:* WATER in the NE, SW and North *Cure: Birdbath with <u>still</u> WATER in the NW* *Enhancement:* WATER in the East or SE *e.g. water fountain, pool, pond, spa, hot tub, or waterfall*
Mountain	*Enhancement:* MOUNTAIN in the East *e.g. boulders, landscape mounds, walls, stone statue or sculpture at least 3 feet tall*
Metal	*Cure:* METAL in the NE, SW, and North *e.g. metal 6-hollow rod wind chimes, door kick plate, planter, pot, statue or sculpture*
Paint	*Cure:* PAINT NW door a blue color or place a blue rug inside or outside
Directions	*Enhancement:* Use doors facing East, SE, South, and West for prosperity *e.g. use these doors frequently*

To Do List

NW 2 and 3 Homes that face **307.6° to 337.5°**
PERIOD 7 (Moved-in Feb 4, 1984 to Feb 3, 2004)

E	SE	S
NE		SW
N	NW	W

Water	*Cure or Remove/Turn Off:* WATER in the SW, NE and South *Enhancement:* WATER in the NW or West *e.g. water fountain, pool, pond, spa, hot tub, or waterfall*
Mountain	*Enhancement:* MOUNTAIN in the West *e.g. boulders, landscape mounds, walls, stone statue or sculpture at least 3 feet tall*
Metal	*Cure:* METAL in the SW and NE *e.g. metal 6-hollow rod wind chimes, door kick plate, planter, pot, statue or sculpture*
Fire	*Cure:* FIRE in the SE and South *e.g. firepit, fireplace, torches, group of candles, red colored rug or paint Southeast-facing doors red*
Directions	*Enhancement:* Use doors facing East, West, and NW *e.g. use these doors frequently*

To Do List

SE	S	SW
E		W
NE	N	NW

NORTH 1 Homes that face **336.6° to 352.5°**
PERIOD 7 (Moved-in Feb 4, 1984 to Feb 3, 2004)

Water	*Cure or Remove/Turn Off:* WATER in the West and SE
	Enhancement: WATER in the North or East
	e.g. water fountain, pool, pond, spa, hot tub, or waterfall
	Enhancement: WATER and FIRE feature good in North
Mountain	*Enhancement:* MOUNTAIN in the NE
	e.g. boulders, landscape mounds, walls, stone statue or sculpture at least 3 feet tall
Metal	*Cure:* METAL in the West and SE
	e.g. metal 6-hollow rod wind chimes, door kick plate, planter, pot, statue or sculpture
Fire	*Cure:* FIRE in the South
	e.g. firepit, fireplace, torches, group of candles, red colored rug or paint South-facing doors red
Directions	*Enhancement:* Use doors facing SW, NW, North, NE and East
	e.g. use these doors frequently

To Do List

SE	S	SW
E		W
NE	N	NW

NORTH 2 and 3 Homes that face **352.6° to 22.5°**
PERIOD 7 (Moved-in Feb 4, 1984 to Feb 3, 2004)

Water	*Cure or Remove/Turn Off:* WATER in the East and NW *Enhancement:* WATER in the South or West *e.g. water fountain, pool, pond, spa, hot tub, or waterfall*
Mountain	*Enhancement:* MOUNTAIN in the SW *e.g. boulders, landscape mounds, walls, stone statue or sculpture at least 3 feet tall*
Metal	*Cure:* METAL in the East and NW *e.g. metal 6-hollow rod wind chimes, door kick plate, planter, pot, statue or sculpture*
Fire	*Cure:* FIRE in the North *e.g. firepit, fireplace, torches, group of candles, red colored rug or paint North-facing doors red*
Directions	*Enhancement:* Use doors facing SE, South, SW, West and NW for prosperity *e.g. use these doors frequently*

To Do List

NE 1 Homes that face **22.6° to 37.5°**
PERIOD 7 (Moved-in Feb 4, 1984 to Feb 3, 2004)

S	SW	W
SE		NW
E	NE	N

Water	*Cure or Remove/Turn Off:* **WATER located in the South, NW and West** *Enhancement:* **WATER in the East** *e.g. water fountain, pool, pond, spa, hot tub, or waterfall*
Mountain	*Enhancement:* **MOUNTAIN in the North** *e.g. boulders, landscape mounds, walls, stone statue or sculpture at least 3 feet tall*
Metal	*Cure:* **METAL in the South, NW and West** *e.g. metal 6-hollow rod wind chimes, door kick plate, planter, pot, statue or sculpture*
Fire	*Cure:* **FIRE in the SW** *e.g. firepit, fireplace, torches, group of candles, red colored rug or paint Southwest-facing doors red*
Directions	*Enhancement:* **Use doors facing NE, SE, East, and North for prosperity** *e.g. use these doors frequently*

To Do List

NE 2 and 3 Homes that face **37.6° to 67.5°**
PERIOD 7 (Moved-in Feb 4, 1984 to Feb 3, 2004)

S	SW	W
SE		NW
E	NE	N

Water	*Cure or Remove/Turn off:* **WATER in the North, SE and East**
	Enhancement: **WATER in the West**
	e.g. water fountain, pool, pond, spa, hot tub, or waterfall
Mountain	*Enhancement:* **MOUNTAIN in the South**
	e.g. boulders, landscape mounds, walls, stone statue or sculpture at least 3 feet tall
Metal	*Cure:* **METAL in the North, SE and East**
	e.g. metal 6-hollow rod wind chimes, door kick plate, planter, pot, statue or sculpture
Fire	*Cure:* **FIRE in the NE**
	e.g. firepit, fireplace, torches, group of candles, red colored rug or paint Northeast-facing doors red
Directions	*Enhancement:* **Use doors facing South, SW, West, and NW for prosperity**
	e.g. use these doors frequently

SW	W	NW
S		N
SE	E	NE

To Do List

EAST 1 Homes that face **67.6° to 82.5°**
PERIOD 7 (Moved-in Feb 4, 1984 to Feb 3, 2004)

Water	**Cure or Remove/Turn Off: WATER in the SW and East** **Enhancement: WATER in the NE or North** *e.g. water fountain, pool, pond, spa, hot tub, or waterfall*
Mountain	**Enhancement: MOUNTAIN in the SE** *e.g. boulders, landscape mounds, walls, stone statue or sculpture at least 3 feet tall*
Metal	**Cure: METAL in the SW and East** *e.g. metal 6-hollow rod wind chimes, door kick plate, planter, pot, statue or sculpture*
Fire	**Cure: FIRE in the East** *e.g. firepit, fireplace, torches, group of candles, red colored rug or paint East-facing doors red*
Directions	**Enhancement: Use doors facing NW, North, NE and SE for prosperity** *e.g. use these doors frequently*

To Do List

SW	W	NW
S		N
SE	E	NE

EAST 2 and 3 Homes that face **82.6° to 112.5°**
PERIOD 7 (Moved-in Feb 4, 1984 to Feb 3, 2004)

Water	*Cure or Remove/*Turn off: WATER in the West and NE *Enhancement:* WATER in the SW or South *e.g. water fountain, pool, pond, spa, hot tub, or waterfall*
Mountain	*Enhancement:* MOUNTAIN in the NW *e.g. boulders, landscape mounds, walls, stone statue or sculpture at least 3 feet tall*
Metal	*Cure:* METAL in the West and NE *e.g. metal 6-hollow rod wind chimes, door kick plate, planter, pot, statue or sculpture* *Cure:* A West-facing door will need both METAL and FIRE if there is a pool in the West
Fire	*Cure:* FIRE in the East and West *e.g. firepit, fireplace, torches, group of candles, red colored rug or paint East and West-facing doors red*
Directions	*Enhancement:* Use doors facing SW, NW, North, SE and South for prosperity *e.g. use these doors frequently*

To Do List

W	NW	N
SW		NE
S	SE	E

SE 1 Homes that face **112.6° to 127.5°**
PERIOD 7 (Moved-in Feb 4, 1984 to Feb 3, 2004)

Water	*Cure or Remove/*Turn Off: WATER in the NW, South and NE *Enhancement:* WATER in the East and North *e.g. water fountain, pool, pond, spa, hot tub, or waterfall*
Mountain	*Enhancement:* MOUNTAIN in SE *e.g. boulders, landscape mounds, walls, stone statue or sculpture at least 3 feet tall*
Metal	*Cure:* METAL in the NW, South and NE *e.g. metal 6-hollow rod wind chimes, door kick plate, planter, pot, statue or sculpture* NOTE: Northwest can have <u>NO</u> FIRE or WATER
Fire	*Cure:* FIRE in the SE *e.g. firepit, fireplace, torches, group of candles, red colored rug or paint Southeast-facing doors red*
Directions	*Enhancement:* Use doors facing West, North, East and SW for prosperity *e.g. use these doors frequently*

To Do List

W	NW	N
SW		NE
S	SE	E

SE 2 and 3 Homes that face **127.6° to 157.5°**
PERIOD 7 (Moved-in Feb 4, 1984 to Feb 3, 2004)

Water	*Cure or Remove/Turn Off:* WATER in the SE, North and SW *Cure:* Bird bath with <u>still</u> WATER in NW *Enhancement:* WATER in the West or South *e.g. water fountain, pool, pond, spa, hot tub, or waterfall*
Mountain	*Enhancement:* MOUNTAIN in the NW *e.g. boulders, landscape mounds, walls, stone statue or sculpture at least 3 feet tall*
Metal	*Cure:* METAL in the SE, North, and SW *e.g. metal 6-hollow rod wind chimes, door kick plate, planter, pot, statue or sculpture* NOTE: Southeast can have <u>NO</u> FIRE or WATER
Paint	*Cure:* PAINT NW-facing door blue, place blue rug (inside or outside) or bird bath with <u>still</u> WATER
Directions	*Enhancement:* Use doors facing West, NE, East, and South for prosperity *e.g. use these doors frequently*

6

Fast Sell: Step-by-Step for Period 8 Homes

Period 8 homes are when the occupants moved in or the home was substantially remodeled between **February 4, 2004 to February 3, 2024.**

This 'period' of time is essential in order to implement the correct Feng Shui for the property. Before you start the *To Do List* recommendations, you will need to do the following:

- Make certain you have the correct move-in date *(Period 8)* if you are in this section of the book.
- Take a compass direction of the property
- Divide the floor plan into 9 sections (tic-tac-toe)
- Write the directions on the outside of floor plan
- Note the *To Do List* adjustments on the floor plan to implement easily

Refer to page 67 to see how to take a compass direction. See page 69 to see how to divide up the floor plan. Refer to pages 70-71 to see where to place the eight directions after locating the facing direction. See the *example on the next page* and implement the recommended adjustments.

NOTE: Place cures first, then the enhancements.

Figure 42: Pools activate energy, see the *To Do List* to make sure the water is properly placed for the home's facing direction.

Here is an **example** of how to implement and apply the Feng Shui for a Period 8, Southwest 2 or 3 house. Notice the bed is placed on the Southeast wall of the master. Install water in the back (Northeast). Place boulders and metal in the front. Desks can face South, NE or North. Living room is arranged to face good directions of Northeast, Southwest and Southeast.

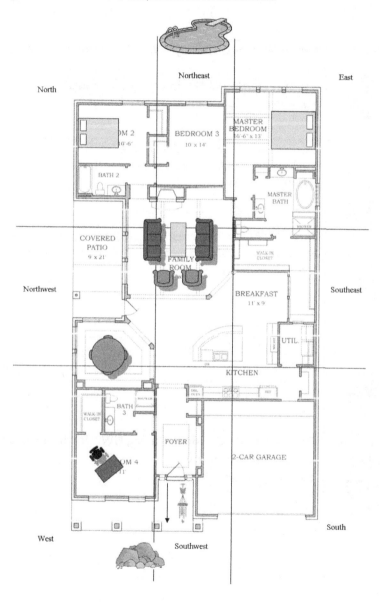

To Do List

NW	N	SE
W		E
SW	S	SE

SOUTH 1 Homes that face **157.6° to 172.5°**
PERIOD 8 (Moved-in Feb 4, 2004 to Feb 3, 2024)

Water	*Cure or Remove/Turn Off:* **WATER in the West and SE** *Enhancement:* **WATER in the North or East** *e.g. water fountain, pool, pond, spa, hot tub, or waterfall*
Mountain	*Enhancement:* **MOUNTAIN in the North** *e.g. boulders, landscape mounds, walls, stone statue or sculpture at least 3 feet tall*
Metal	*Cure:* **METAL in the West and SE** *e.g. metal 6-rod wind chimes, door kick plate, planter, pot, statue or sculpture*
Fire	*Cure:* **FIRE in the South** *e.g. firepit, fireplace, torches, group of candles, red colored rug or paint South-facing doors red*
Directions	*Enhancement:* **Use doors facing NW, North, NE, East and SW for prosperity** *e.g. use these doors frequently*

To Do List

NW	N	SE
W		E
SW	S	SE

SOUTH 2 and 3 Homes that face **172.6° to 202.5°**
PERIOD 8 (Moved-in Feb 4, 2004 to Feb 3, 2024)

Water	***Cure or Remove/Turn Off:*** **WATER in the East and NW** ***Cure:*** **Pool located in North <u>is</u> a cure (can also add FIRE)** ***Enhancement:*** **WATER in the South or West** *e.g. water fountain, pool, pond, spa, hot tub, or waterfall* ***Enhancement:*** ***WATER and FIRE feature good in*** **South**
Mountain	***Enhancement:*** **MOUNTAIN in the South** *e.g. boulders, landscape mounds, walls, stone statue or sculpture at least 3 feet tall*
Metal	***Cure:*** **METAL in the East and NW** *e.g. metal 6-rod wind chimes, door kick plate, planter, pot, statue or sculpture*
Fire	***Cure:*** **FIRE in the North** *e.g. firepit, fireplace, torches, group of candles, red colored rug or paint North-facing doors red*
Directions	***Enhancement:*** **Use doors facing NE, SE, South, SW and West for prosperity** *e.g. use these doors frequently*

To Do List

N	NE	E
NW		SE
W	SW	S

SW 1 Homes that face **202.6° to 217.5°**
PERIOD 8 (Moved-in Feb 4, 2004 to Feb 3, 2024)

Water	*Cure or Remove/Turn Off:* **WATER in the NE and West** *Enhancement:* **WATER in the SW or South** *e.g. water fountain, pool, pond, spa, hot tub, or waterfall*
Mountain	*Enhancement:* **MOUNTAIN in the NE** *e.g. boulders, landscape mounds, walls, stone statue or sculpture at least 3 feet tall*
Metal	*Cure:* **METAL in the NE** *e.g. metal 6-rod wind chimes, door kick plate, planter, pot, statue or sculpture*
Fire	*Cure:* **Fire in the East** *e.g. firepit, fireplace, torches, group of candles, red colored rug*
Directions	*Enhancement:* **Use doors facing North, SE, South, SW and NW for prosperity** *e.g. use these doors frequently*

To Do List

SW 2 and 3 Homes that face **217.6° to 247.5°**
PERIOD 8 (Moved-in Feb 4, 2004 to Feb 3, 2024)

N	NE	E
NW		SE
W	SW	S

Water	*Cure or Remove/Turn Off:* WATER in the SW and East *Enhancement:* WATER in the NE or North *e.g. water fountain, pool, pond, spa, hot tub, or waterfall*
Mountain	*Enhancement:* MOUNTAIN in the SW *e.g. boulders, landscape mounds, walls, stone statue or sculpture at least 3 feet tall*
Metal	*Cure:* METAL in the SW and East *e.g. metal 6-rod wind chimes, door kick plate, planter, pot, statue or sculpture*
Fire	*Cure:* Fire in the West *e.g. firepit, fireplace, torches, group of candles, red colored rug*
Directions	*Enhancement:* Use doors that face North, NE, SE, South and NW for prosperity. *e.g. use these doors frequently*

NE	E	SE
N		S
NW	W	SW

To Do List

WEST 1 Homes that face **247.6° to 262.5°**
PERIOD 8 (Moved-in Feb 4, 2004 to Feb 3, 2024)

Water	*Cure or Remove/Turn Off:* WATER in the South, West and NW *Enhancement:* WATER in the East *e.g. water fountain, pool, pond, spa, hot tub, or waterfall*
Mountain	*Enhancement:* MOUNTAIN in the East *e.g. boulders, landscape mounds, walls, stone statue or sculpture at least 3 feet tall*
Metal	*Cure:* METAL in the West, South and NW *e.g. metal 6-rod wind chimes, door kick plate, planter, pot, statue or sculpture*
Fire	*Cure:* FIRE in the SW *e.g. firepit, fireplace, torches, group of candles, red colored rug*
Directions	*Enhancement:* Use doors facing NE, East, SE and North for prosperity *e.g. use these doors frequently*

To Do List

NE	E	SE
N		S
NW	W	SW

WEST 2 and 3 Homes that face **262.6° to 292.5°**
PERIOD 8 (Moved-in Feb 4, 2004 to Feb 3, 2024)

Water	*Cure or Remove/Turn Off:* WATER in the East, North and SE *Cure:* Bird bath with <u>still</u> WATER in the NE (or "FIRE" as noted below) **Enhancement:** WATER in West *e.g. water fountain, pool, pond, spa, hot tub, or waterfall*
Mountain	*Enhancement:* MOUNTAIN in the West *e.g. boulders, landscape mounds, walls, stone statue or sculpture at least 3 feet tall*
Metal	*Cure:* METAL in the East, North and SE *e.g. metal 6-rod wind chimes, door kick plate, planter, pot, statue or sculpture* *Cure:* METAL and FIRE in the East if there is a pool there
Fire	*Cure:* FIRE in the NE (or <u>still</u> water bird bath as noted above in "WATER") *e.g. firepit, fireplace, torches, group of candles, red colored rug or paint East-facing doors red*
Directions	*Enhancement:* Use doors facing South, SW, West or NW for prosperity *e.g. use these doors frequently*

To Do List

E	SE	S
NE		SW
N	NW	W

NW 1 Homes that face **292.6° to 307.5°**
PERIOD 8 (Moved-in Feb 4, 2004 to Feb 3, 2024)

Water	*Cure or Remove/Turn Off:* WATER in the North, West and NE *Cure:* Bird bath with <u>still</u> WATER in the East *Enhancement:* WATER in the SE or NW *e.g. water fountain, pool, pond, spa, hot tub, or waterfall*
Mountain	*Enhancement:* MOUNTAIN in the NW *e.g. boulders, landscape mounds, walls, stone statue or sculpture at least 3 feet tall*
Metal	*Cure:* METAL in the North, West and NE *e.g. metal 6-rod wind chimes, door kick plate, planter, pot, statue or sculpture*
Fire	*Cure:* FIRE in the East (or <u>still</u> water bird bath as noted above in "WATER") *e.g. firepit, fireplace, torches, group of candles, red colored rug* NOTE: NW-facing doors should not be a red color
Directions	*Enhancement:* Use doors that face SE, South, SW, or NW for prosperity *e.g. use these doors frequently*

To Do List

E	SE	S
NE		SW
N	NW	W

NW 2 and 3 Homes that face **307.6° to 337.5°**
PERIOD 8 (Moved-in Feb 4, 2004 to Feb 3, 2024)

Water 	*Cure or Remove/Turn Off:* WATER in the South, East and SW *Cure:* Bird bath with <u>still</u> WATER in the West (or "FIRE" as noted below) *Enhancement:* WATER in the NW or SE *e.g. water fountain, pool, pond, spa, hot tub, or waterfall*
Mountain 	*Enhancement:* MOUNTAIN in the SE *e.g. boulders, landscape mounds, walls, stone statue or sculpture at least 3 feet tall*
Metal 	*Cure:* METAL in the South, East and SW *e.g. metal 6-rod wind chimes, door kick plate, planter, pot, statue or sculpture*
Fire 	*Cure:* FIRE in the West (or <u>still</u> water bird bath as noted above in "WATER") *e.g. firepit, fireplace, torches, group of candles, red colored rug* **NOTE: NW-facing doors should not be a red color**
Directions 	*Enhancement:* Use doors that face SE, NW, North and NE for prosperity *e.g. use these doors frequently*

To Do List

NORTH 1 Homes that face **337.6° to 352.5°**
PERIOD 8 (Moved-in Feb 4, 2004 to Feb 3, 2024)

SE	S	SW
E		W
NE	N	NW

Water	*Cure or Remove/Turn Off:* WATER in the SE, West and NW *Cure:* Bird bath with <u>still</u> WATER in the SW (or "FIRE" as noted below) *Enhancement:* WATER in the North, South or NE *e.g. water fountain, pool, pond, spa, hot tub, or waterfall*
Mountain	*Enhancement:* MOUNTAIN in the North *e.g. boulders, landscape mounds, walls, stone statue or sculpture at least 3 feet tall*
Metal	*Cure:* METAL in the SE, West and NW *e.g. metal 6-rod wind chimes, door kick plate, planter, pot, statue or sculpture*
Fire	*Cure:* FIRE in the SW (or <u>still</u> water bird bath as noted above in "WATER") *e.g. firepit, fireplace, torches, group of candles, red colored rug* *Enhancement:* FIRE in the South and/or North *e.g. firepit, fireplace, torches, group of candles, red colored rug or paint North or South-facing doors red*
Directions	*Enhancement:* Use doors that face South, North, NE and East for prosperity *e.g. use these doors frequently*

To Do List

NORTH 2 and 3 Homes that face **52.6° to 22.5°**
PERIOD 8 (Moved-in Feb 4, 2004 to Feb 3, 2024)

SE	S	SW
E		W
NE	N	NW

Water	*Cure or Remove/Turn Off:* **WATER in the NW, East and SE** *Cure:* **Bird bath with <u>still</u> WATER in the NE (or "FIRE" as noted below)** *Enhancement:* **WATER in the South, North or SW** *e.g. water fountain, pool, pond, spa, hot tub, or waterfall*
Mountain	*Enhancement:* **MOUNTAIN in the South** *e.g. boulders, landscape mounds, walls, stone statue or sculpture at least 3 feet tall*
Metal	*Cure:* **METAL in the NW, East and SE** *e.g. metal 6-rod wind chimes, door kick plate, planter, pot, statue or sculpture*
Fire	*Cure:* **FIRE in the NE (or <u>still</u> water bird bath as noted above in "WATER")** *e.g. firepit, fireplace, torches, group of candles, red colored rug* *Enhancement:* **FIRE in the North and/or South** *e.g. firepit, fireplace, torches, group of candles, red colored rug or paint North or South-facing doors red*
Directions	*Enhancement:* **Use doors that face South, SW, West, and North for prosperity** *e.g. use these doors frequently*

To Do List

S	SW	W
SE		NW
E	NE	N

NE 1 Homes that face **22.6° to 37.5°**
PERIOD 8 (Moved-in Feb 4, 2004 to Feb 3, 2024)

Water	*Cure or Remove/Turn Off:* **WATER in the SW and SE** *Cure:* **Bird bath with <u>still</u> WATER in the South (or "FIRE" as noted below)** *Enhancement:* **WATER in the NE or NW** *e.g. water fountain, pool, pond, spa, hot tub, or waterfall*
Mountain	*Enhancement:* **MOUNTAIN in the SW** *e.g. boulders, landscape mounds, walls, stone statue or sculpture at least 3 feet tall*
Metal 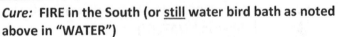	*Cure:* **METAL in the SW and SE** *e.g. metal 6-rod wind chimes, door kick plate, planter, pot, statue or sculpture*
Fire	*Cure:* **FIRE in the South (or <u>still</u> water bird bath as noted above in "WATER")** *e.g. firepit, fireplace, torches, group of candles, red colored rug*
Directions	*Enhancement:* **Use doors that face West, NW, North, NE and East for prosperity** *e.g. use these doors frequently*

To Do List

S	SW	W
SE		NW
E	NE	N

NE 2 and 3 Homes that face **37.6° to 67.5°**
PERIOD 8 (Moved-in Feb 4, 2004 to Feb 3, 2024)

Water	*Cure or Remove/Turn Off:* **WATER in the NE and NW** *Cure:* **Bird bath with <u>still</u> WATER in the North (or "FIRE" as noted below)**
	Enhancement: **WATER in the SW or SE** *e.g. water fountain, pool, pond, spa, hot tub, or waterfall*
Mountain	*Enhancement:* **MOUNTAIN in the NE** *e.g. boulders, landscape mounds, walls, stone statue or sculpture at least 3 feet tall*
Metal	*Cure:* **METAL in the NE and NW** *e.g. metal 6-rod wind chimes, door kick plate, planter, pot, statue or sculpture*
Fire	*Cure:* **FIRE in the North (or <u>still</u> water bird bath as noted above in "WATER")** *e.g. firepit, fireplace, torches, group of candles, red colored rug*
Directions	*Enhancement:* **Use doors that face South, SW, West, East or SE for prosperity** *e.g. use these doors frequently*

To Do List

SW	W	NW
S		N
SE	E	NE

EAST 1 Homes that face **67.6° to 82.5°**
PERIOD 8 (Moved-in Feb 4, 2004 to Feb 3, 2024)

Water	*Cure or Remove/Turn Off:* WATER in the NW, South and NE *Cure:* Bird bath with <u>still</u> WATER in the SE (or "FIRE" as noted below) *Enhancement:* WATER in the East or North *e.g. water fountain, pool, pond, spa, hot tub, waterfall*
Mountain	*Enhancement:* MOUNTAIN in the East *e.g. boulders, landscape mounds, walls, stone statue or sculpture at least 3 feet tall*
Metal	*Cure:* METAL in the NW, South and NE *e.g. metal 6-rod wind chimes, door kick plate, planter, pot, statue or sculpture*
Fire	*Cure:* FIRE in the SE (or <u>still</u> water bird bath as noted above in "WATER") *e.g. firepit, fireplace, torches, group of candles, red colored rug*
Directions	*Enhancement:* Use doors that face SW, West, North, and East for prosperity *e.g. use these doors frequently*

To Do List

SW	W	NW
S		N
SE	E	NE

EAST 2 and 3 Homes that face **82.6° to 112.5°**
PERIOD 8 (Moved-in Feb 4, 2004 to Feb 3, 2024)

Water 	*Cure or Remove/Turn Off:* WATER in the SE, North and SW *Cure:* Bird bath with <u>still</u> WATER in the NW *Enhancement:* WATER in the West or South *e.g. water fountain, pool, pond, spa, hot tub, or waterfall*
Mountain 	*Enhancement:* MOUNTAIN in the West *e.g. boulders, landscape mounds, walls, stone statue or sculpture at least 3 feet tall*
Metal 	*Cure:* METAL in the Southeast, North and SW *e.g. metal 6-rod wind chimes, door kick plate, planter, pot, statue or sculpture*
Fire	*Enhancement:* FIRE in the West *e.g. firepit, fireplace, torches, group of candles, red colored rug or paint West-facing doors red*
Directions	*Enhancement:* Use doors that face West, NE, East, and South for prosperity *e.g. use these doors frequently*

To Do List

W	NW	N
SW		NE
S	SE	E

SE 1 Homes that face **112.6° to 127.5°**
PERIOD 8 (Moved-in Feb 4, 2004 to Feb 3, 2024)

Water	*Cure or Remove/Turn Off:* **WATER in the East, South and North** *Enhancement:* **WATER in the NW** *e.g. water fountain, pool, pond, spa, hot tub, or waterfall*
Mountain	*Enhancement:* **MOUNTAIN in the SE** *e.g. boulders, landscape mounds, walls, stone statue or sculpture at least 3 feet tall*
Metal 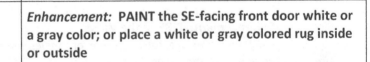	*Cure:* **METAL in the East, South and North** *e.g. metal 6-rod wind chimes, door kick plate, planter, pot, statue or sculpture*
Paint	*Enhancement:* **PAINT the SE-facing front door white or a gray color; or place a white or gray colored rug inside or outside**
Directions	*Enhancement:* **Use doors that face West, NW, NE, SE and SW for prosperity** *e.g. use these doors frequently*

To Do List

SE 2 and 3 Homes that face **127.6° to 157.5°**
PERIOD 8 (Moved-in Feb 4, 2004 to Feb 3, 2024)

W	NW	N
SW		NE
S	SE	E

Water 	*Cure or Remove/Turn Off:* WATER in the West, North and South *Enhancement:* WATER in the SE *e.g. water fountain, pool, pond, spa, hot tub, or waterfall*
Mountain 	*Enhancement:* MOUNTAIN in the NW *e.g. boulders, landscape mounds, walls, stone statue or sculpture at least 3 feet tall*
Metal 	*Cure:* METAL in the West, North and South *e.g. metal 6-rod wind chimes, door kick plate, planter, pot, statue or sculpture*
Fire 	*Enhancement:* FIRE or WATER in the SE *e.g. firepit, fireplace, torches, group of candles, red colored rug or paint Southeast-facing doors red*
Directions	*Enhancement:* Use doors that face NW, NE, East, SE and SW for prosperity *e.g. use these doors frequently*

7

Fast Sell: Step-by-Step for Period 9 Homes

*Period 9 homes are when the occupants moved in or the home was substantially remodeled between **February 4, 2024 to February 3, 2044**.*

This 'period' of time is essential in order to implement the correct Feng Shui for the property. Before you start the *To Do List* recommendations, you will need to do the following:

- Make certain you have the correct move-in date *(Period 9)* if you are in this section of the book.
- Take a compass direction of the property
- Divide the floor plan into 9 sections (tic-tac-toe)
- Write the directions on the outside of floor plan
- Note the *To Do List* adjustments on the floor plan to implement easily

Refer to page 67 to see how to take a compass direction. See page 69 to see how to divide up the floor plan. Refer to pages 70-71 to see where to place the eight directions after locating the facing direction. See the *example on the next page* and implement the recommended adjustments.

NOTE: Place cures first, then the enhancements.

Figure 40: In order to proceed you will need the move-in date and an accurate compass direction of the house.

Here is an **example** of how to implement and apply the Feng Shui for a Period 9, West 2 or 3 house. Notice the bed is placed on the South wall of the master. Install water in the back (East). Place wind chimes in the NE. Desks can face SW, SE, or East. Living room is arranged to face good directions of West, East, and South.

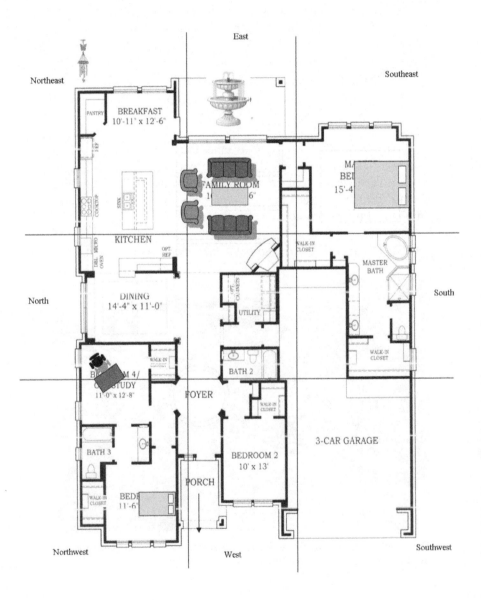

To Do List

NW	N	SE
W		E
SW	S	SE

SOUTH 1 Homes that face **157.6° to 172.5°**
PERIOD 9 (Moved-in Feb 4, 2024 to Feb 3, 2044)

Water	*Cure or Remove/Turn Off:* WATER in the SE, West and NW *Cure:* Birdbath with <u>still</u> WATER in the SW *Enhancement:* WATER in the South, North or NE *e.g. water fountain, pool, pond, spa, hot tub, waterfall* *Enhancement:* South can have WATER/FIRE feature
Mountain	*Enhancement:* MOUNTAIN in the South, NE or North *e.g. boulders, landscape mounds, walls, stone statue or sculpture at least 3 feet tall*
Metal	*Cure:* METAL in the SE, West and NW *e.g. metal 6-rod wind chimes, door kick plate, planter, pot, statue or sculpture*
Fire	*Enhancement:* FIRE in the South (and/or "WATER" noted above)* *e.g. firepit, fireplace, torches, group of candles, red colored rug or paint South-facing doors red*
Directions	*Enhancement:* Use doors facing South, North, NE and East* *e.g. use these doors frequently*

To Do List

NW	N	SE
W		E
SW	S	SE

SOUTH 2 and 3 Homes that face **172.6° to 202.5°**
PERIOD 9 (Moved-in Feb 4, 2024 to Feb 3, 2044)

Water 	*Cure Remove/Turn Off:* WATER in the NW, East and SE *Cure:* Birdbath with <u>still</u> WATER in the NE *Enhancement:* WATER in the North, South or SW *e.g. water fountain, pool, pond, spa, hot tub, waterfall* *Enhancement:* North can have WATER/FIRE feature
Mountain 	*Enhancement:* MOUNTAIN in the North, SW or South *e.g. boulders, landscape mounds, walls, stone statue or sculpture at least 3 feet tall*
Metal 	*Cure:* METAL in the NW, East and SE *e.g. metal 6-rod wind chimes, door kick plate, planter, pot, statue or sculpture*
Fire 	*Enhancement:* FIRE in the North (and/or "WATER" noted above) *e.g. firepit, fireplace, torches, group of candles, red colored rug or paint door(s)*
Directions 	*Enhancement:* Use doors facing North, South, SW and West *e.g. use these doors frequently*

To Do List

N	NE	E
NW		SE
W	SW	S

SW 1 Homes that face **202.6° to 217.5°**
PERIOD 9 (Moved-in Feb 4, 2024 to Feb 3, 2044)

Water	*Cure or Remove/Turn Off:* **WATER in the NW, South and NE** *Enhancement:* **WATER in the SW, East or North** *e.g. water fountain, pool, pond, spa, hot tub, waterfall* *Enhancement:* **SW can have WATER/FIRE feature**
Mountain	*Enhancement:* **MOUNTAIN in the North, SW or East** *e.g. boulders, landscape mounds, walls, stone statue or sculpture at least 3 feet tall*
Metal	*Cure:* **METAL in the NW, South and NE** *e.g. metal 6-rod wind chimes, door kick plate, planter, pot, statue or sculpture*
Fire	*Cure:* **FIRE in the NE** *e.g. firepit, fireplace, torches, group of candles, red colored rug or paint door(s)* *Cure:* **Door in NE needs FIRE and METAL**
Directions	*Enhancement:* **Use doors facing SW, North, East and West** *e.g. use these doors frequently*

To Do List

SW 2 and 3 Homes that face **217.6° to 247.5°**
PERIOD 9 (Moved-in Feb 4, 2024 to Feb 3, 2044)

N	NE	E
NW		SE
W	SW	S

Water	*Cure or Remove/Turn Off:* WATER in the SE, North and SW *Enhancement:* WATER in the NE, West or South *e.g. water fountain, pool, pond, spa, hot tub, waterfall* *Enhancement:* NE can have WATER/FIRE feature
Mountain	*Enhancement:* MOUNTAIN in the NE, North or West *e.g. boulders, landscape mounds, walls, stone statue or sculpture at least 3 feet tall*
Metal	*Cure:* METAL in the SE, North and SW *e.g. metal 6-rod wind chimes, door kick plate, planter, pot, statue or sculpture*
Fire 	*Cure:* FIRE in the SW *e.g. firepit, fireplace, torches, group of candles, red colored rug or paint door(s)* *Cure:* Door in SW needs FIRE and METAL
Directions	*Enhancement:* Use doors facing NE, East, South, and West *e.g. use these doors frequently*

To Do List

NE	E	SE
N		S
NW	W	SW

WEST 1 Homes that face **247.6° to 262.5°**
PERIOD 9 (Moved-in Feb 4, 2024 to Feb 3, 2044)

Water	*Cure or Remove/Turn Off:* WATER in the SW and SE *Cure:* Birdbath with <u>still</u> water in South *Enhancement:* WATER in the West, NE or NW *e.g. water fountain, pool, pond, spa, hot tub, waterfall* *Enhancement:* West can have WATER/FIRE feature
Mountain	*Enhancement:* MOUNTAIN in the West, NW or NE *e.g. boulders, landscape mounds, walls, stone statue or sculpture at least 3 feet tall*
Metal	*Cure:* METAL in the SW and SE *e.g. metal 6-rod wind chimes, door kick plate, planter, pot, statue or sculpture*
Fire	*Enhancement:* FIRE in the West (can have FIRE/WATER feature) *e.g. firepit, fireplace, torches, group of candles, red colored rug or paint door(s)*
Directions	*Enhancement:* Use doors facing NE, East, West, NW and North *e.g. use these doors frequently*

To Do List

NE	E	SE
N		S
NW	W	SW

WEST 2 and 3 Homes that face **262.6° to 292.5°**
PERIOD 9 (Moved-in Feb 4, 2024 to Feb 3, 2044)

Water	*Cure or Remove/Turn Off:* Water feature located in the NE, NW and West *Cure:* Birdbath with <u>still</u> water in North *Enhancement:* WATER in the East, SE or SW *e.g. water fountain, pool, pond, spa, hot tub, waterfall*
Mountain	*Enhancement:* MOUNTAIN in the East, SE or SW *e.g. boulders, landscape mounds, walls, stone statue or sculpture at least 3 feet tall*
Metal	*Cure:* METAL in the NE, NW and West *e.g. metal 6-rod wind chimes, door kick plate, planter, pot, statue or sculpture*
Fire	*Enhancement:* FIRE in the East (can have FIRE/WATER feature) *e.g. firepit, fireplace, torches, group of candles, red colored rug or paint door(s)*
Directions	*Enhancement:* Use doors facing East, SE, South, SW and West *e.g. use these doors frequently*

To Do List

E	SE	S
NE		SW
N	NW	W

NW 1 Homes that face **292.6° to 307.5°**
PERIOD 9 (Moved-in Feb 4, 2024 to Feb 3, 2044)

Water	*Cure or Remove/Turn Off:* WATER in the South, NW and West *Cure:* Birdbath with <u>still</u> water in SW *Enhancement:* WATER in the SE or East *e.g. water fountain, pool, pond, spa, hot tub, waterfall* *Enhancement:* SE can have WATER/FIRE feature
Mountain	*Enhancement:* MOUNTAIN in the SE or East *e.g. boulders, landscape mounds, walls, stone statue or sculpture at least 3 feet tall*
Metal	*Cure:* METAL in the South, NW and West *e.g. metal 6-rod wind chimes, door kick plate, planter, pot, statue or sculpture*
Fire	*Enhancement:* FIRE in the SE *e.g. firepit, fireplace, torches, group of candles, red colored rug or paint door(s)*
Directions	*Enhancement:* Use doors facing East, SE, North and NE *e.g. use these doors frequently*

To Do List

NW 2 and 3 Homes that face **307.6° to 337.5°**
PERIOD 9 (Moved-in Feb 4, 2024 to Feb 3, 2044)

E	SE	S
NE		SW
N	NW	W

Water 	*Cure or Remove/Turn Off:* WATER in the North, SE and East *Cure:* Birdbath with <u>still</u> WATER in the NE *Enhancement:* WATER in the NW or West *e.g. water fountain, pool, pond, spa, hot tub, waterfall*
Mountain 	*Enhancement:* MOUNTAIN in the NW or West *e.g. boulders, landscape mounds, walls, stone statue or sculpture at least 3 feet tall*
Metal 	*Cure:* METAL in the North, SE and East *e.g. metal 6-rod wind chimes, door kick plate, planter, pot, statue or sculpture*
Fire 	<u>DO NOT</u> locate any FIRE in the NW *e.g. firepit, fireplace, torches, group of candles, red colored rug or paint door(s)*
Directions 	*Enhancement:* Use doors facing NW, SW, West and South *e.g. use these doors frequently*

To Do List

NORTH 1 Homes that face **337.6° to 352.5°**
PERIOD 9 (Moved-in Feb 4, 2024 to Feb 3, 2044)

SE	S	SW
E		W
NE	N	NW

Water	*Cure or Turn Off/Relocate:* WATER in the SW and East *Cure:* Birdbath with <u>still</u> WATER in the West *Enhancement:* WATER in the South, NE or North *e.g. water fountain, pool, pond, spa, hot tub, waterfall*
Mountain	*Enhancement:* MOUNTAIN in the South, North or NE *e.g. boulders, landscape mounds, walls, stone statue or sculpture at least 3 feet tall*
Metal	*Cure:* METAL in the SW and East *e.g. metal 6-rod wind chimes, door kick plate, planter, pot, statue or sculpture*
Fire	*Enhancement:* FIRE in the South (can have FIRE/WATER feature) *e.g. firepit, fireplace, torches, group of candles, red colored rug or paint door(s)*
Directions	*Enhancement:* Use doors facing South, NE, North and NW *e.g. use these doors frequently*

To Do List

SE	S	SW
E		W
NE	N	NW

NORTH 2 and 3 Homes that face **352.6° to 22.5°**
PERIOD 9 (Moved-in Feb 4, 2024 to Feb 3, 2044)

Water	*Cure:* **Birdbath with <u>still</u> WATER in the East** *Enhancement:* **WATER in the South, SW or North** *e.g. water fountain, pool, pond, spa, hot tub, waterfall* *Enhancement:* **North can have WATER/FIRE feature**
Mountain	*Enhancement:* **MOUNTAIN in the North, South or SW** *e.g. boulders, landscape mounds, walls, stone statue or sculpture at least 3 feet tall*
Metal 	*Cure:* **METAL in the NE and West** *e.g. metal 6-rod wind chimes, door kick plate, planter, pot, statue or sculpture*
Fire	*Enhancement:* **FIRE in the North (can have FIRE/WATER feature)** *e.g. firepit, fireplace, torches, group of candles, red colored rug or paint door(s)*
Directions	*Enhancement:* **Use doors facing South, SW, NW and North** *e.g. use these doors frequently*

To Do List

S	SW	W
SE		NW
E	NE	N

NE 1 Homes that face **22.6° to 37.5°**
PERIOD 9 (Moved-in Feb 4, 2024 to Feb 3, 2044)

Water	*Cure or Remove/*Turn off: WATER in the West and SE *Cure:* Birdbath with <u>still</u> WATER in the South *Enhancement:* WATER in the SW, North or East *e.g. water fountain, pool, pond, spa, hot tub, waterfall*
Mountain	*Enhancement:* MOUNTAIN in the SW, North or East *e.g. boulders, landscape mounds, walls, stone statue or sculpture at least 3 feet tall*
Metal	*Cure:* METAL in the West and SE *e.g.* metal 6-rod wind chimes, door kick plate, planter, pot, statue or sculpture
Fire	*Enhancement:* FIRE in the SW (can have FIRE/WATER feature) *e.g. firepit, fireplace, torches, group of candles, red colored rug or paint door(s)*
Directions	*Enhancement:* Use doors facing SW, North, NW, NE and East *e.g. use these doors frequently*

To Do List

S	SW	W
SE		NW
E	NE	N

NE 2 and 3 Homes that face **37.6° to 67.5°**
PERIOD 9 (Moved-in Feb 4, 2024 to Feb 3, 2044)

Water	*Cure or Remove/Turn Off:* WATER in the East and NW *Cure:* Birdbath with <u>still</u> WATER in the North *Enhancement:* WATER in the NE, North or East *e.g. water fountain, pool, pond, spa, hot tub, waterfall* *Enhancement:* NE can have WATER/FIRE feature
Mountain	*Enhancement:* MOUNTAIN in the NE, South or West *e.g. boulders, landscape mounds, walls, stone statue or sculpture at least 3 feet tall*
Metal	*Cure:* METAL in the East *e.g. metal 6-rod wind chimes, door kick plate, planter, pot, statue or sculpture*
Fire 	*Enhancement:* FIRE in the NE (can have FIRE/WATER feature) *e.g. firepit, fireplace, torches, group of candles, red colored rug or paint door(s)*
Directions	*Enhancement:* Use doors facing South, SW, West, NE and SE *e.g. use these doors frequently*

To Do List

SW	W	NW
S		N
SE	E	NE

EAST 1 Homes that face **67.6° to 82.5°**
PERIOD 9 (Moved-in Feb 4, 2024 to Feb 3, 2044)

Water	*Cure or Remove/Turn Off:* **WATER in the East, South and North** *Enhancement:* **WATER in the West, NW or NE** *e.g. water fountain, pool, pond, spa, hot tub, waterfall* *Enhancement:* **West can have WATER/FIRE feature**
Mountain	*Enhancement:* **MOUNTAIN in the West, NW or NE** *e.g. boulders, landscape mounds, walls, stone statue or sculpture at least 3 feet tall*
Metal	*Cure:* **METAL in the East, South and North** *e.g. metal 6-rod wind chimes, door kick plate, planter, pot, statue or sculpture* **East door MUST be cured with Metal and CANNOT have any Fire**
Fire	*Enhancement:* **FIRE in the West (can have FIRE/WATER feature)** *e.g. fireplt, fireplace, torches, group of candles, red colored rug or paint West-facing doors red*
Directions	*Enhancement:* **Use doors facing West, NW, NE and SE** *e.g. use these doors frequently*

To Do List

SW	W	NW
S		N
SE	E	NE

EAST 2 and 3 Homes that face **82.6° to 12.5°**
PERIOD 9 (Moved-in Feb 4, 2024 to Feb 3, 2044)

Water 	*Cure or Remove/Turn Off:* WATER in the West, North and South *Enhancement:* WATER in the East, SE or SW *e.g. water fountain, pool, pond, spa, hot tub, waterfall* *Enhancement:* East can have WATER/FIRE feature
Mountain	*Enhancement:* MOUNTAIN in the East, SW or SE *e.g. boulders, landscape mounds, walls, stone statue or sculpture at least 3 feet tall*
Metal	*Cure:* METAL in the West, North and South *e.g. metal 6-rod wind chimes, door kick plate, planter, pot, statue or sculpture*
Fire	*Enhancement:* FIRE in the East (can have FIRE/WATER feature) *e.g. firepit, fireplace, torches, group of candles, red colored rug or paint South-facing doors red*
Directions	*Enhancement:* Use doors facing SW, NW, NE, East and SE *e.g. use these doors frequently*

To Do List

W	NW	N
SW		NE
S	SE	E

SE 1 Homes that face **112.6° to 127.5°**
PERIOD 9 (Moved-in Feb 4, 2024 to Feb 3, 2044)

Water	*Cure or Remove/Turn Off:* WATER in the NE, SW and North
	Cure: WATER in the NW (pool or bird bath)
	Enhancement: WATER in the SE or East
	e.g. water fountain, pool, pond, spa, hot tub, waterfall
	Enhancement: SE can have WATER/FIRE feature
Mountain	*Enhancement:* MOUNTAIN in the SE or East
	e.g. boulders, landscape mounds, walls, stone statue or sculpture at least 3 feet tall
Metal	*Cure:* METAL in the NE, SW and North
	e.g. metal 6-rod wind chimes, door kick plate, planter, pot, statue or sculpture
Fire	*Enhancement:* FIRE in the SE (can have FIRE/WATER feature)*
	e.g. fireplt, fireplace, torches, group of candles, red colored rug or paint door(s)
Directions	*Enhancement:* Use doors facing West, East, SE and South
	e.g. use these doors frequently

To Do List

W	NW	N
SW		NE
S	SE	E

SE 2 and 3 Homes that face **127.6° to 157.5°**
PERIOD 9 (Moved-in Feb 4, 2024 to Feb 3, 2044)

Water	*Cure or Remove/Turn Off:* WATER in the SW, NE and South *Cure:* Birdbath with <u>still</u> WATER in the SE *Enhancement:* WATER in the NW and West *e.g. water fountain, pool, pond, spa, hot tub, waterfall*
Mountain	*Enhancement:* MOUNTAIN in the NW or West *e.g. boulders, landscape mounds, walls, stone statue or sculpture at least 3 feet tall*
Metal	*Cure:* METAL in the SW, NE and South *e.g. metal 6-rod wind chimes, door kick plate, planter, pot, statue or sculpture*
Fire	**DO NOT put FIRE in the NW**
Directions	*Enhancement:* Use doors facing NW, West, and East *e.g. use these doors frequently*

8

Space Clearing

There are dozens if not hundreds of ways to clear a home or property of stagnant energy. When you're ready to sell your home, space clearing helps prepare your home and property for a successful sale.

Clearing a property can be complex or simple. *We prefer simple*. Yes, even the simple method involves a few steps and gathering some materials.

The clearing items can be easily obtained online or at metaphysical stores. You will need about an hour to do the process/clearing depending on the size of the home.

Arrive with a grateful heart and good intentions. The intention here is to announce to the home that you are working together to create a welcoming environment for the new owners who will love and care for the property as well as releasing the current owners with gratitude for the time they owned and cared for the home.

You can do the energy clearing yourself or hire someone to do this process for you. The choice is yours. If there has been any disturbance, unrest or undesirable events (ghosts, natural death, violence or murder) at the property, it is probably best to have a professional space clearing.

Figure 43: Metal singing bowls will dispel negative or stagnant energy.

You will need:

A metal singing bowl or metal bell. You can also download and play a YouTube recording of metal singing bowl tones on your smartphone, but an actual metal singing bowl or bell is preferable.

A sage stick to burn along with a lighter. Have a bowl to catch the falling embers. Use a large feather for moving the smoke or mist around the space. You may also use a sage mist spray.

Incense to burn or spray mist fragrance; rose and jasmine are great choices since they are very high vibrationally.

The Process

1. Come to the clearing ceremony freshly bathed or showered and wearing fresh clothes.

2. Begin your clearing ceremony at the front door of the home.

3. Say a prayer requesting assistance to protect you as the energy of the home is cleared completely during this ceremony, to raise its vibration, and welcome the new owners (or whatever the purpose of this clearing is).

4. Ring the metal singing bowl or the metal bell three times to awaken the energy. These vibrational tones will announce your request for assistance in clearing all stagnant, negative energy. Make an appeal to clear and raise the vibrational frequency of the home and property.

5. Walk *clockwise* in every room of the house while ringing the metal bowl or bell. This action will loosen and release stagnant energy so that it transforms. If your bowl or bell makes a thud sound, you have encountered a very dense, negative energy. Continue to ring the bell or bowl until it releases. The thud will turn to a beautiful ringing sound. When complete, return to the front door.

6. Now, light the sage stick or have your sage spray mist bottle in hand.

7. Announce that you are now clearing all stagnate negative energy from the home. Have some soothing music playing in the background to reset the frequency.

8. Repeat the process of going to each room in a *clockwise* direction with your sage or spray mist. Use the feather to scatter the smoke from the sage. Keep a clear intention to clear stagnant, negative, and lingering energies.

9. The third and final *clockwise* pass in all rooms will be with a fragrant spray or incense. Rose oil extract has the highest vibration (320 megahertz). Mix water and a small amount of rose or jasmine essential oil in a spray bottle. Burning beautiful, fragrant incense will also lift the energy.

10. At this juncture of the space clearing, speak words and blessings with high, vibrational energy such as: *love, peace, harmony, bliss, good health, prosperity, joy, kindness,* and *generosity.*

11. After returning to the front door, thank the house and the energies within the house for responding so graciously to this process. Bless them with love and gratitude.

12. Next, if there is a backyard, walk it with a lighted incense stick around the perimeter in a *clockwise* manner. During the process, give thanks to the 'landlords of the land' for allowing the occupants to live in the home in peace. If appropriate ask them to assist in attracting the new owners of the property.

13. You can leave the incense burning in a safe place outside until it is fully extinguished.

14. Repeat the process for the front yard. Walk with a lighted incense stick around the perimeter in a *clockwise* manner. Express gratitude and give thanks to the 'landlords of the land' for allowing the occupants to live there in peace and harmony. If appropriate ask them to assist in attracting the new owners of the property.

15. You can leave the incense burning in a safe place in the front yard until it is fully extinguished.

After this process, it is respectful to continue burning incense safely outside the home periodically (weekly or monthly). This honors the 'landlords of the land.' These unseen energies occupy the space outside the home, and they appreciate being acknowledged.

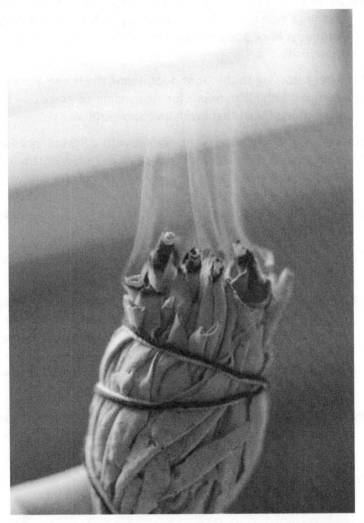

Figure 44: Sage burning is an ancient ritual known also as smudging. Other benefits believed to be associated with sage when burned are giving wisdom, clarity, and increasing spiritual awareness.

Ghosts and Spirits in a Home

If you're a real estate agent or Feng Shui consultant long enough, you will likely encounter ghosts or spirits at some point in your career. There are many reasons that ghosts will occupy or haunt a home. Most often the spirit has a history with the property and cannot let it go. The home may have a DEL (see page 47), or the home may be located next to a graveyard or church. And another common reason is the home has been sitting empty for an extended period of time.

Denise, one of the authors, tells of experience she had with a client in Phoenix, Arizona.

"A couple I consult with in Phoenix, Arizona bought a mid-century house. They soon discovered that a ghost was present. It was a female ghost that had a 50-year history with the house. After the woman died, her son inherited the property. He tried to keep tenants for over three years, but they all left because of the ghost. All the renters would get frightened even though the ghost was not evil, nor did it play tricks on them. He finally decided to sell; this is when my clients bought the house.

I was invited to Feng Shui the home and do an energy space clearing because of its history. When I made contact with the spirit, she told me that her life there was extremely happy and she couldn't bear to leave. When I explained to her that her beloved husband and other family members were waiting for her, she relented. She also confessed that she liked the couple that bought the house and approved of their remodeling plans."

As real estate agents, your particular state laws may require that you must disclose a house has a ghost if you have been informed by the homeowners. A professional energy space clearing can take care of this.

9

Affirmations for Success in Real Estate

The next two chapters will introduce you to aspects of selling and buying properties that successful real estate agents are beginning to address with their clients.

This is certainly a personal decision and something you should be comfortable offering. We find that most clients are open to these suggestions and are pleased that they have found a real estate agent who takes such a personal and holistic approach in selling their home or locating a new home.

If the following information is already incorporated into your life, you most likely attract situations and clients who understand how valuable these tools are. Openly sharing this information with each other is an opportunity for us to encourage and empower one another. The positive ripple effects are profound.

Some of you may say, "I've tried affirmations and they do not work!" Most affirmations are ineffective because the language is crafted to target the conscious level of the mind. This is the reasoning part of the brain, and certain affirmations will cause an internal argument with yourself. This is called cognitive dissonance and it creates resistance to manifestations.

For example, with each positive declaration, your conscious mind may say 'that's not true!" This internal conflict uses up precious energy and can actually create the reverse of what is desired. Since everything is energy, we constantly emit energetic frequencies through our thoughts, actions, and emotions. Learning how to use this energy in a positive way is essential.

Read more about the *Law of Attraction* and how to work in concert with the conscious and subconscious mind in Chapter 10. Meanwhile, the following affirmations and prayers will help shift your energy to experience better results.

There are several types of affirmations and affirmative prayers in this chapter that will help you or your client sell or buy a home. There are others that are designed to attract money and wealth.

Please note that we honor all faiths. So, use the elements of these prayers and craft them to fit your particular faith. The prayers/affirmations are largely written in first person with additional individuals noted in parenthesis when applicable. You will want to include others, such as your family, spouse or partner, who will be living in the property or affected by the purchase into your prayer. Feel free to add anything specific to your needs and requirements or create your own unique prayers and affirmations.

For the best results, say your affirmations/prayers when you first wake up and again when drifting off to sleep. These are the times of day that the subconscious mind is most receptive to new ideas and concepts. You can say your affirmations during the day as well, just remember these two, very important times when the mind is most responsive. Be prepared to be awed.

Figure 45: Prayer is *not* begging. Your prayer, which is a mental act, must be accepted as an image in your mind before the power of the subconscious can make it productive.

Sell a House
Two Affirmations

Infinite Intelligence attracts to me the buyer for this home who wants it and who will be nurtured and prospered by it. This buyer is being sent to me by Divine Design, which makes no mistakes. This buyer may look at many other homes, but mine is the only one he/she wants and will buy because they are guided by the Infinite Intelligence within them. I know the buyer is right, the time is right, and the price is right. Everything about it is right. The deeper currents of my subconscious mind are now in operation bringing both of us together in Divine order. I know that it is so. Thank you.

Buy a Home
Affirmation Detailed

It is extremely helpful to write a list of amenities and qualities you would like this property to have. If there is more than one occupant of the home, it is helpful for this to be a collaborative adventure. Review these daily during the home buying process while imagining and feeling the amenities as though you were already enjoying them. Remember, you can always revise this from time to time. For example, "Our new home has a…"

- Welcoming curb appeal and entry
- Gourmet kitchen area where friends and family can cordially gather...I can hear the laughter and feel the joy
- Master bedroom that inspires rest, relaxation and rejuvenation (personalize this for your desires)

Envision your offer accepted, house keys being handed to you and easily moving into your ideal dream home.

You get the idea...
- List YOUR desires
- Envision them *(especially first thing in the morning and right before drifting off to sleep)*
- Sense them as though they already exist
- Repeat daily while expressing gratitude

Buy a Home
Affirmative Prayer

Heavenly Father-Mother God *(or your faith salutation here)*, Thank you for the opportunity to purchase a home that fully supports me (and my family or my partner, etc.) physically, emotionally, mentally and spiritually. Divinely guide me (us) and my real estate agent to the best home, in the location, at the time and the price that serves the highest outcome for all concerned. Inspire and empower me (us) to equally bless this home, property and neighborhood (area) while living there in peace, harmony, prosperity, love, and joy.

Bless the previous homeowner(s) and occupants. Guide them to completely and thoroughly release the home and property physically, emotionally and spiritually so that the home and property welcomes, recognizes and honors me (us) as its new owner(s) and occupants.

Thank you for being ever present and orchestrating every detail of this transaction so that it flows smoothly. I (we) declare that all is in Divine Order. Give me (us) wisdom and understanding throughout this process so that I (we) make good decisions. Thank you that this is done in the name and through the nature of the living Christ Jesus and so it is. Amen (or however you choose to close your prayer).

Buy Investment Property
Affirmation Detailed

This is where you write your financial goals, along with how you envision utilizing the property. You can include others who will be an integral part of your vision. Just make sure everyone is on the same page and envisioning the same outcome. You can revise these as you receive new insights.

For example:
- Great location
- Good value
- Growth potential
- Positive cash flow within "X" months/years

You get the idea here...
- List YOUR desires
- Envision them *(especially first thing in the morning and right before drifting off to sleep)*
- Sense them as though they already exist
- Repeat daily while expressing gratitude

Buy Investment Property
Affirmative Prayer

Heavenly Father-Mother God *(or your faith salutation here),* Thank you for the ability to purchase an investment property that serves my (our) investment goals. Guide me (us) and my (our) real estate agent to the property/building/land (state the kind of property here) that will be mutually beneficial to everyone involved in this transaction who will be served by this property now and for years to come.

Give me vision to see the possibilities within this property that can be achieved and still provide a highly profitable return on investment. Show me its highest and best use. Give me wisdom, understanding and guidance to choose wisely and make good decisions.

Use this property to bless everyone who is ever involved with, offices at, or lives in (customize this to identify the property use) this property. Thank you that this is done in the name and through the nature of the living Christ Jesus...and so it is. Amen (or however you choose to close your prayer).

One Sentence Affirmations

All that is mine by Divine Right is now released and reaches me in perfect ways under grace.

I am undisturbed by appearances. I trust in God and He now brings to me the desire of my heart.

I now have the single eye of the Spirit and see only completion.

Hunches are my hounds of Heaven—they lead me in the perfect way.

My supply comes from God, and big happy financial surprises now come to me, under grace, in perfect ways.

Thy Kingdom is come, Thy Will is done in, through and around me.

Peace and prosperity reign within these walls; failure is transmuted into success, lack into plenty and discord into peace.

The 55 x 5 Affirmation

This is a unique Law of Attraction manifestation technique, and it works great! Basically, the goal of this method is to reprogram the thought patterns of the subconscious mind. Over a consecutive 5-day period you can change your thoughts which have a direct link to your energetic frequency. This energetic frequency is how we manifest things in our life. In other words, the 55 X 5 technique is a way to raise the energetic frequencies around us that help us attract whatever we want.

The process: Choose an affirmation (short and direct is best), handwrite it 55 times for 5 days. It must be handwritten, not typed on your computer. Do only one affirmation at a time.

Choose affirmations so you will not argue that the statement is not true or *feel* it isn't true. For example, you may question "I close on 5 homes a month!" If this is not believable to you, and your feelings broadcast otherwise, then you will cancel out the possibility. Reframe it by saying *"I'm in the process of* closing on 5 homes per month." Handwrite it 55 times for 5 days. Then let it go. Trust that the Law of Attraction is unfolding and orchestrating all that needs to happen to bring about your desire.

Figure 46: In order for this method to work effectively, you must hand write your affirmation. This creates a direct link to the brain.

A Multi-Million Dollar Prayer

A spiritual business magnate told Dr. Joseph Murphy *(author of The Power of Your Subconscious Mind)* that he became a multimillion-dollar success with thousands of employees by saying the following affirmative prayer every morning and night.

"I recognize the eternal source of all riches which never fails. I am divinely guided in all my ways, and I adapt myself to all new ideas. Infinite Intelligence is constantly revealing to me better ways to serve my fellow man. I am guided and directed to create products that will bless and help humanity. I attract men and women who contribute to the peace, prosperity, and progress of our business. I am an irresistible magnet and attract fabulous wealth by giving the best possible quality of products and services.

I am constantly in tune with the Infinite and the substance of wealth. Infinite Intelligence governs all my plans and purposes, and I predicate all my success on the truth that God leads, guides, and governs all my undertakings. I am at peace inwardly and outwardly at all times. I am a tremendous success.

I am one with God, and God is always successful. I must succeed. I am succeeding now. I radiate love and goodwill to all those around me and to all my employees. I fill my mind and heart with God's love, power, and energy. All those connected with me are spiritual links to my growth, welfare, and prosperity. I give all honor and glory to God."

Affirmations for Wealth

I like money. I love it! I use it wisely, constructively, and judiciously. Money is constantly circulating in my life. I release it with joy, and it returns to me multiplied in a wonderful way. It is good and very good. Money flows to me in avalanches of abundance. I use it for good only, and I am grateful for my good and for the riches of my mind.

I am one with infinite riches of my subconscious mind. It is my right to be rich, happy, and successful. Money flows to me freely, copiously, and endlessly. I am forever conscious of my true value. I give my talents freely, and I am wonderfully blessed financially. It is wonderful!

Figure 47: Use these affirmations right before falling asleep and upon awakening to attract more wealth.

Importance of Intentions

Barbara shares the following story about a Feng Shui consultation for a client in California regarding clear intention and affirmative prayer:

"One of the reasons for the consultation was to provide more visibility for my client's business. The color red was needed. A temporary adjustment was placed until the client identified just the right item to place in the location that I recommended. A month later the client called in a panic to say that chaos had erupted in her business. As a master make-up artist, she had written a best-selling book that was routinely purchased by high-profile plastic surgeons to distribute to their clients. Two large orders had been abruptly canceled with no explanation. I asked the client if she had made any adjustments since her consultation. The client said, 'Nothing except replacing the item that you said needed to be red. I replaced it with a beautiful red mask.'

I asked questions about the mask's origin and determined it was safe yet obviously powerful. Then I asked what was said to the mask when it was placed as the adjustment and the client said, 'I just put it there because Barbara told me to.' Quickly I wrote out an affirmative prayer to bless the mask and restore harmony to my client's business, emailed it to my client. She said the blessing and gave the mask its role in her business. By that afternoon both orders were restored and one even doubled their order. Crisis averted!"

When making the adjustments recommended for a particular property, be sure you clearly intend that these adjustments are creating your intended result...selling quickly, bringing prosperity and harmony for all concerned. You can speak the prayer of affirmation out loud, or simply by visualizing the intended outcome. You will find suggestions in Chapters 7, 8, 9, and 10 that will resonate with your style.

10

The Law of Attraction

Many of you know, utilize and can validate the wonderful results of working in concert with the Law of Attraction.

You know that this 'law' attracts what you focus on. If you focus on positive results, you attract positive outcomes. Focus on negative results, you attract and multiply those.

Michael J. Losier, the Law of Attraction How-To Guru, says it this way, "I attract to my life whatever I give my attention, energy and focus to, whether positive or negative."

The Law of Attraction is very much like Feng Shui in that it is in operation whether you believe in it or not. However, when you consciously use these methods to co-create your reality, you elevate the possibilities to a whole new level.

Many books emerged on the subject, or various aspects of the subject, such as the best-seller by Dr. Joseph Murphy, Ph.D., *The Power of Your Subconscious Mind*. And the popular book, *Law of Attraction: The Science of Attracting More of What You Want and Less of What You Don't*, by Michael J. Losier that has sold over 3 million copies and has been translated into 35 languages.

Figure 48: We attract 'things' to us by our thoughts. Repeated thoughts accompanied by strong emotions can happen quickly. Constant worry about no money coupled with negative images/feelings will attract a lack of funds or clients. *So, what DO you want?! Focus and attract that!*

The Conscious and Subconscious Minds

The movie, *The Secret*, as well these books and others on this subject changed the way we view our thoughts and perhaps even more importantly, that our thoughts can actually create! Our subconscious mind and conscious mind are not two different minds. No indeed. They are simply two distinct functions of the brain with very different operating systems.

Our conscious mind is in charge of reasoning things out. For example, we choose our mates, the house we will live in, what we will do for a living, and so forth. This is the brilliance of the reasoning brain – it can make decisions. It is proficient in its function; we decide all the time.

The *subconscious* mind takes care of thousands of body functions that you do not have to think about. This operating system behind the scenes handles the digestive system, heart, circulation of the blood, breathing, and much more without any conscious choice made by you.

The subconscious mind accepts what it is regularly fed and impressed on it. This is especially true with deeply charged emotions. It is like a bed of soil that accepts any kind of seed— good or bad.

It is also unique in that it does not process the words, "no" "not" and "don't." For example, you may adamantly say, "I don't want that." Then, two days later the exact thing you steadfastly stated you "don't want" showed up.

The *essential element* here is to focus on what you *do want!*

Now that we know that, we want to 'feed' and program our subconscious mind to create our desires. Thoughts and feelings/emotions are energy, frequency, and vibrations. In order to manifest what we want, we will need to change 'our story.'

This new frequency/story will attract what we want—it is the law. Yes, the law; the *law of attraction*. This is how things are created in our 3rd dimension world. It is simply how energy works. Call it quantum physics, the quantum field, string theory, the law of attraction, God, love frequency, holographic principles, the zone, affirmative prayer—it is all the same wonderful energy!

We, in fact, manifest things (good and bad) in our life all the time, most of the time by default. This is done by observing or the cycle of observation. We observe what we receive. While observing, we create a vibration/signal. The Law of Attraction responds to the signal. We get *more* of what we observe. See the Observation Cycle on the next page to better understand how this works.

Figure 49: Abundance and wealth can mean money, loving relationships, excellent health, opportunities, freedom or a combination of any of these.

Observation Cycle
(This is non-deliberate or by-default Attraction)

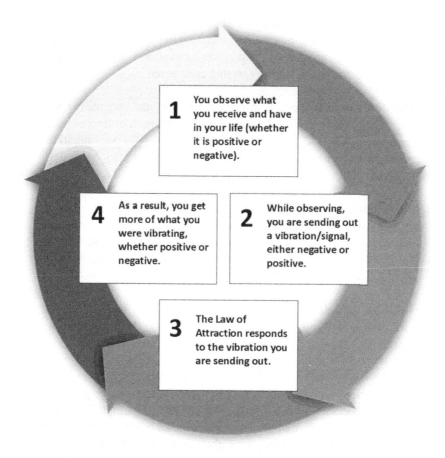

1 You observe what you receive and have in your life (whether it is positive or negative).

4 As a result, you get more of what you were vibrating, whether positive or negative.

2 While observing, you are sending out a vibration/signal, either negative or positive.

3 The Law of Attraction responds to the vibration you are sending out.

This image is the Observation Cycle from the *Law of Attraction* book by Michael J. Losier. We recreated its likeness here with his permission. The cycle demonstrates how we observe what is in our life such as work, relationships, money, health, and so on. As a result, our observations create a feeling/vibration/signal that can either be negative or positive.

Using the Law of Attraction in Real Estate

Deliberately manifesting what we want in our life is key. So, the question becomes, 'What do you want to achieve?' Do you want this house to sell and satisfy all parties? Do you see happy buyers entering the home and envisioning themselves living there happily-ever-after? Do you envision a successful, harmonious transaction for everyone concerned?

When preparing a home to be listed for sale, do you meet with clients and offer them methods for preparing themselves and their home for sale? Or are you trying to hold the positive expectations for everyone without allowing them to be active participants in this meaningful process?

In this book we have presented many techniques that we know are successful. Feel free to personalize them and make them your own or use our checklists provided throughout the book. Be the real estate agent who makes a lasting, positive difference in your clients' lives.

How can this be achieved? Imagine that someone calls and criticizes something about your listing. It may be the location, the fact that it is on a corner lot and not an interior lot, the size of the backyard, or it has no curb appeal.

Where does your mind go? Do you immediately go into defensive mode? Do you think, "Oh no, not this again."? Or do you objectively consider the information and realize that you are one person closer to finding the right buyer for the property?

Perhaps you are asking, "Isn't this just "positive thinking"? Yes and no. Does it require positive thinking? Yes. Is that enough? No.

Have you ever said something positive and not believed what you were saying? We all have. That produces a conflicting vibration and typically produces mixed or unwanted results as we have previously discussed.

For example, when envisioning a successful sale, which of the following statements do you think will be a more effective affirmation?

1. I love knowing that the right buyers who are fully qualified for this property, find and are attracted to this property in perfect timing.
2. It is sometimes hard to get financing for a home and I hope that the qualified buyers will find this home.

You can easily see that the first statement broadcasts clear, positive vibrations. It is so important to become very cognizant of the message you are sending out. You want to achieve the highest possible results.

The following are some ideas of how you can reset your thoughts and words.

1. Identify what you want
2. Give attention, energy and focus to what you want
3. Allow

You probably know what you want and can craft the best wording to express that desire. If you don't know exactly what you DO want, then identify what you DON'T want and choose the opposite of that. Now, that was easy!

CONTRAST vs CLARITY

Don't Want	Do Want
Unqualified buyer	Qualified buyer
Home with bad Feng Shui	Home with good Feng Shui
"What DON'T you want?"	*"What DO you want?"*

You may also know how to give attention, energy and focus to what you want. This can include daily visualizations, taking action to promote the property while holding wonderful thoughts about the outcome, as well as observing the great qualities of the property, the current owners, and the buyers.

Doing your affirmations, prayers, and visualizations in a drowsy state such as when you are just waking or falling asleep is a great idea. This is when the subconscious mind is most receptive to new ideas.

Allowing the Desire to Manifest

Do you know how to ALLOW your desired outcomes to manifest? This is perhaps the *most important ingredient* and the least understood. It is the process that removes all doubt so that the manifestation is allowed to come into being.

Simply put:
- Strong desire with strong doubt = no manifestation
- Strong desire with little doubt = slow manifestation
- Strong desire with no doubt = quick manifestation

The following is a story that Barbara shares about a Law of Attraction realization. Perhaps you can relate.

"Having dinner with a dear mentor and friend, I shared something I wanted to manifest. She offered suggestions about how that might be accomplished which included others being involved in the process. Like a petulant child I said, 'No, I want to do it myself!' To which my friend responded, 'Well, that explains why that hasn't manifested yet.' Ouch!"

Yes, remaining open to options and out-of-the-box thinking can serve us very well in the allowing process.

Another friend's story is a good example of allowing, yet also about being specific in stating our desire. This friend wanted to manifest a specific set of china. To her amazement, someone gave her six place settings of the exact china pattern she had been visualizing. She was truly amazed until she fully unpacked the box and realized that most of the pieces were either chipped or cracked. She knew that was not what she visualized and she was initially very disappointed.

However, she knew that she had received EVIDENCE that the Law of Attraction was working and she got more specific about her "order." She became so excited because she received evidence. Now she knew beyond any doubt that her manifestation was very close. Soon, twelve place settings of flawless china in the pattern she had been imagining were gifted to her by someone who had no idea what she had been visualizing. And, her manifestation doubled from her initial "evidence."

The big lesson in these stories is to *know* exactly what you want and *visualize* the result clearly and in detail. Remove your limiting beliefs, words and actions. If doubt creeps in, thank it for sharing and send it away. Reset your vibration to faith and trust while noticing "evidence."

Figure 50: Celebrate your 'evidence' that the Law of Attraction is working for you!

Denise, one of the authors of this book, used the visualization method, strong belief (no doubts) and a clear intention to get a literary agent and publisher for her first Feng Shui book many years ago. She sent out over 400 query letters to literary agents in the U.S., Canada, and U.K. Over the course of a year, she received over 300 rejection letters. Not discouraged, she regularly visualized her book on the *Barnes & Noble* bookshelves; saw herself at book signings and being interviewed on television and radio about her book.

She even had a dear friend tell her that, in this day and age, she would *never* get a literary agent. Denise did not listen and wrote it off as nonsense. She decided, "That is her belief, not mine!" Finally, after 12 months, she got a call from an interested literary agent. She had a book deal a month later with Llewellyn Worldwide. Llewellyn went on to publish two more of her books. She never gave up or lost faith that her book would be published. She is now the author of eleven very successful Feng Shui books!

Watch Your Thoughts

It is said that we have about 60,000 thoughts a day. Now you don't need to monitor all of thoughts (impossible anyway) but start by noticing and replacing the negative ones with positive ones to assure your success. For example, below are words, thoughts and feelings that can repel money and success.

- Saying I can't afford
- Saying, believing and feeling that money is dirty
- Saying, believing and feeling that money is the root of all evil
- Saying, believing and feeling jealousy for those with more money or more accomplishments than you

These are what you DON'T want, so ask yourself, "What DO I want?" State those and frame them in positive statements.

In the Cycle of Observation, notice that we can create by default. The goal is to consciously create. This means that we must catch and replace negative thoughts to avoid being easily "programmed" by the news, social media, or accept beliefs from other "authority" figures.

Most of our beliefs were passed down to us and we accepted them as fact. By reprogramming our subconscious mind, we can consciously determine what we create. By observing and appreciating the EVIDENCE, we start a positive cycle of intentional manifestation. Now, that's an observation cycle we all want to be on!

"The first step to getting what you want is to have the courage to get rid of what you don't."

—Zig Ziglar

11

Releasing Blocks to Success

In the previous chapter, we discussed ways to manifest and attract what we want. Now we will learn ways to remove energies that can block your manifestations.

Barbara, one of the authors, has worked with and is mentored by Michael Losier, the author of the *Law of Attraction*. While collaborating they noticed that sometimes manifestations seemed to get 'stuck' for no apparent reason.

During this time, Michael was introduced to *The Emotion Code®* and shared his experience with Barbara. Soon they learned that there were times when trapped emotions and energies *could* limit manifestations. What a breakthrough!

The Emotion Code is a book written by Dr. Bradley Nelson where he describes a method to release the energies of trapped emotions because they cause imbalance in the body and can impede your success and wellbeing. In the newly edited version, transformational strategist Tony Robbins has written the forward and endorsed the system.

This energetic healing system has a multitude of useful, everyday applications including selling homes. How is that possible? Can you think of a time when buying and selling homes is *without* emotion?!

The Emotion Code method was discovered through prayer, Divine guidance and practical application. During Dr. Nelson's 17-year holistic medical practice, he had a sincere desire to help his patients on a deeper level. With the permission of his patients, he intentionally connected to their subconscious mind to seek answers that were stored within them. As he asked a series of questions, he was able to discern either a 'yes' or 'no' answer through muscle testing. This uncovered information about emotions that had become trapped in various parts of their bodies.

Once the emotions are identified, they are released by moving a magnet over the central meridian from the front of the head to the back several times. There are many YouTube videos that demonstrate this simple and powerful process.

Why connect to the subconscious mind? Our subconscious mind is the storage facility for every memory, trauma and event in our lives. It even stores generational memories. By learning to tap into the precious resource, we are able to accomplish things once believed to be impossible.

By opening our minds and hearts to broader avenues of assistance, not only does it support us individually it can also expand out to touch humanity as a whole.

The image below provides a glimpse of what is available when we tap into *all* our resources.

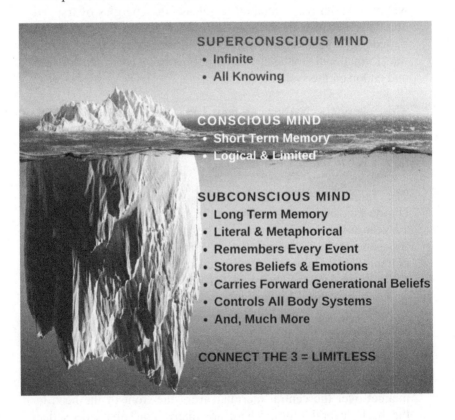

SUPERCONSCIOUS MIND
- Infinite
- All Knowing

CONSCIOUS MIND
- Short Term Memory
- Logical & Limited

SUBCONSCIOUS MIND
- Long Term Memory
- Literal & Metaphorical
- Remembers Every Event
- Stores Beliefs & Emotions
- Carries Forward Generational Beliefs
- Controls All Body Systems
- And, Much More

CONNECT THE 3 = LIMITLESS

Figure 51: The subconscious mind is infinite in its depth. It is like a quantum supercomputer!

Barbara, who is a certified Emotion Code practitioner, relates the following experience using this process for selling a client's home.

"Several years ago, I was contacted by a physician whose home had been on the market for more than two years. She and her husband had already relocated to another city, so they were ready to move on with their lives. She was familiar with Feng Shui and requested my assistance in getting the property sold.

The property was located several hundred miles from me, so I arranged a video call with her real estate agents to view the property. As I video-toured the property I noticed that the property was empty except for a few decorative items until we came to a room that had a mattress and bedding in it.

The kitchen cabinets were also very taste-specific but certainly not the reason the home had not sold in over two years. Additionally, the overall Feng Shui of the home was not the issue and it was priced right, so I was a bit perplexed.

After noticing the bedding, I asked if there was a house-sitter and they explained that one of the owners stayed there when he was in town finalizing the sale of his business. He had evidently been doing this since they vacated the home almost two years prior.

Having recently learned the Emotion and Body Codes (the more advanced energetic healing system also created by Dr. Nelson), I had a hunch that this was not a Feng Shui issue, but an emotional attachment. While these systems were developed to work on people and animals, I decided to try them on the home. I knew it couldn't hurt, so I proceeded with my experiment.

During the session I discovered that not only was the husband attached to this beautiful custom home that he and his wife had built and happily lived in for many years, the home was attached to him. How could this be?

As stated earlier in the book, scientists now know that *everything* in our universe is energy. Homes too are energy and in their ideal state, they protect and support us. They can absorb and broadcast positive or negative energy. Homes are 'aware' if they are loved or resented.

In fact, I rented a home that I loved and cared for dearly for several years. When I moved out all the appliances, HVAC and electrical systems quit working as soon as a new family moved in. It was as though the house threw a temper-tantrum. But I digress...

We have all walked into homes where kind, loving, responsible families have raised their children, and are ready to downsize. It is very evident when the property has been well-maintained and the home well-loved. There are other homes where you can feel the tension in the air as soon as you walk through the door. Only to discover later, that the home had domestic disharmony.

So, what do you do?

In my client's case there were some trapped emotions in both the husband and the home which I released. Then, I lovingly communicated to the home and released its' attachment to the owners. I explained to the lovely home that I knew it did not want to be alone and empty with no life in it! Together, the home and I raised the energy of the property through prayer and intention to attract the ideal owners who would love and care for it.

Right after this the homeowners decided to refinish the kitchen cabinets, the husband removed all personal possessions and I energetically cleared the space. The home was taken off the market briefly while they made these improvements.

Within two weeks of putting it back on the market, the home sold. Everyone was thrilled and amazed at the quick results."

Since this experience Barbara has assisted many sellers and real estate agents to successfully sell homes that had stagnated on the market. She has also learned that it is so much more productive to address these potential issues when a home is being listed for sale. Why wait for it to linger on the market?!

Can you do this process yourself? Yes, with a little bit of training and effort. You can learn to treat a home as a sentient being, connect to it energetically, and determine what is required through muscle testing.

Muscle testing is simple and straightforward to learn. However, it does take practice. It is also very easy to learn how to connect to people, homes and seemingly inanimate objects. Again, it takes practice. But soon you will begin to trust the answers you receive.

In this book, we are not teaching "how to muscle test." Please refer to our video tutorial at www.RealEstateFengShuiSeries.com or YouTube instructional videos that teach this easy-to-learn process. There are several different methods and you will find one that works comfortably for you. It will be well worth the effort to master muscle testing.

Another practical use of muscle testing is determining the best furniture and décor placement for staging a property to sell. Using muscle testing, you can ask if it is best for an item to be utilized in the room that you are decorating or staging. If the answer is 'yes' then you can muscle test for the specific location in the room until you get a 'yes' for best placement. You will also find it helpful when determining the most supportive direction to place your desk or design your workspace.

This technique aligns perfectly with the Eight Mansions Feng Shui system that gives the best directions for individuals based on their birth date.[1] We find that people will test 'no' for negative facing directions and 'yes' for positive facing directions. At that point, you have confirmation that you are better supported by arranging surroundings that are more positive for you and your clients.

---

[1] To learn more about the Eight Mansion system, refer to the book *Feng Shui That Rocks the House* by Denise Liotta-Dennis.

Remember, you will need to learn how to phrase questions so that they can be answered by a simple 'yes' or 'no' when using muscle testing. For example, "Is this the best placement for my desk to face so that I am fully supported in my work?" Or, "Is this the best placement to optimize the sale of this home?" Obviously, when you get 'no' answers, you keep going until you identify the 'yes' response.

Whether staging a home, reorganizing your office, or selling a home, you will find that applying the processes shared here can provide truly amazing results!

This is exactly why we wanted to include this chapter in the book. While helping people with either buying or selling their properties, it is good to make use of many tools.

The Emotion Code book is available at all major booksellers such as Barnes & Noble and online stores such as Amazon. Excellent videos are available at www.DiscoverHealing.com that further explains this incredible process. This website also has a free online introductory course to learn muscle testing.

The following page shows the official *Emotion Code Chart*™ provided with permission from Dr. Bradley Nelson. This is the chart used to discover Trapped Emotions by the muscle testing process. When the trapped energies are identified you proceed to release them by using the technique explained in *The Emotion Code* book.

Next, you will discover another new tool called the "818 Light Codes" that can be used to fill the void created after releasing trapped emotions and energies.

 DISCOVER HEALING

The Emotion Code Chart

	A	B
1 HEART OR SMALL INTESTINE	Abandonment Betrayal Forlorn Lost Love Unreceived	Effort Unreceived Heartache Insecurity Overjoy Vulnerability
2 SPLEEN OR STOMACH	Anxiety Despair Disgust Nervousness Worry	Failure Helplessness Hopelessness Lack of Control Low Self-Esteem
3 LUNG OR COLON	Crying Discouragement Rejection Sadness Sorrow	Confusion Defensiveness Grief Self-Abuse Stubbornness
4 LIVER OR GALL BLADDER	Anger Bitterness Guilt Hatred Resentment	Depression Frustration Indecisiveness Panic Taken for Granted
5 KIDNEYS OR BLADDER	Blaming Dread Fear Horror Peeved	Conflict Creative Insecurity Terror Unsupported Wishy Washy
6 GLANDS OR SEXUAL ORGANS	Humiliation Jealousy Longing Lust Overwhelm	Pride Shame Shock Unworthy Worthless

The 818 Light Codes

At the same time Barbara was being certified as an Emotion Code Practitioner, she encouraged a friend, Debbie Johnstone, to also go through the certification. They each practiced the method on each other and began realizing that while they were proficient in releasing and removing trapped energies, it seemed that something should be placed in the void where those negative energies once resided.

Debbie, who is a Phoenix-based animal communicator after retiring from a 20-year corporate IT career, started to receive black and white symmetrical images. At the time, she had no idea that they even had a purpose other than to amuse her during meditation. A few years later, those simple images evolved into beautiful, colorful geometric shapes and patterns. As individual images arrived, she realized that each one had a specific purpose.

At this point, Debbie and Barbara began to wonder if these images were just the higher energetic vibration needed to install where the previous lower energies had been removed. So, they began to experiment. To their amazement they were witnessing rapid positive results when used in conjunction with *The Emotion Code* process for people, animals and properties.

We have included a few of the beautiful black and white images in the next few pages. These are useful with home sales and buying. They are quite easy to use. Simply gaze at the image, breathe it in, then send it out through your breath asking that it be installed into the person, animal or object with Divine Love, activated and anchored by the Breath of God (Holy Spirit).

The colored images will be available *The Real Estate Feng Shui Series'* website at www.RealEstateFengShuiSeries.com. You can find the entire collection of images at www.818LightCodes.com.

Clear Resistant Energy

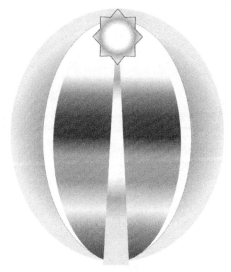

Prosperity

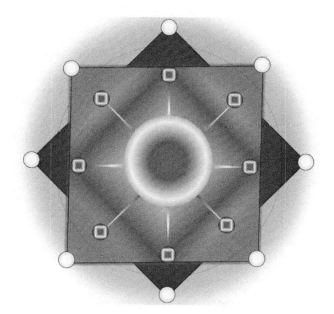

Opening to Receive

Acceleration

12

Professional Wrap Up!

Now you are ready to put all your new tools to work for you and your clients!

That Was Easy

Your Feng Shui Toolbox in Chapter 4 along with the correct *To Do List* in Chapters 5, 6 or 7 for each property provides you a never before available guide to produce quicker sales and satisfied clients.

This truly is your handbook for ushering in a new level of expertise for your real estate career and/or your investing portfolio. You will want it to be your constant companion to refer to often.

Each property you assess, adjust and enhance will provide feedback. Pay attention to that feedback. You will gain a competence and confidence in every aspect of this process as you apply your new skills.

The *Seller's and Buyer's Feng Shui Checklists* on pages 62 and 63 provide an example of the Action Items to easily incorporate in your sales strategy. The *Property Checklist* (page 64) used in conjunction with the *Step-by-Step Feng Shui Guide* (page 65) and the correct property *To Do List* will keep you focused.

Practice each phase of the processes you have been shown throughout this book until you feel competent with each of the steps. Each step is dependent on the others. Used together you will experience remarkable results.

As you experience the outcomes of utilizing these new tools, you will know that you have truly served your clients with the highest degree of care and professionalism.

It is our absolute joy to offer this compendium of ancient knowledge to you in the modern convenience of a readily available handbook. We have done the calculations for you so that you are not required to memorize hundreds of complex formulas.

Many fortunate blessings to each of you and the lives you enrich!

Bonus

Classical Feng Shui Techniques

*Deeper insights into the world of
Classical Feng Shui systems and practices*

The origins of Feng Shui date back thousands of years; some sources say it began around 4000 B.C. Kan Yu is the old term for Feng Shui. In fact, the term *Feng Shui* has only been in use for a little more than a hundred years since the Ching Dynasty. The golden era of Feng Shui occurred during the Tang Dynasty between the seventh and tenth centuries A.D.

Over time, two main branches of practice emerged, *San He* and *San Yuan.* These ideologies form the foundation of Classical Feng Shui. It is important to understand that Feng Shui is highly dynamic and constantly developing, even today. Most modern-day Feng Shui masters will combine these schools into one huge body of knowledge.

All Feng Shui systems share a common set of principles and theories. For example, all schools refer to the principles of yin-yang, the Five Elements, the Ba Gua, and the four factors—direction, occupants, time, and location. San He and San Yuan both use a Chinese compass known as a Luo Pan in order to consider the landforms and topography.

These two approaches differ slightly on emphasis. The San He School places importance on examining form, shape, contour, appearance, flow, and confirmation whereas San Yuan places its focus on time; it considers the influence, qualities and types of chi and time dimension. Even though the strategies of these ideologies are slightly different, the objectives are the same. And that is to examine the energy of the site using form, shape, direction, timing, a compass, and the individual themselves that will rent, own, occupy, or develop the property.

San He System

San He, also known as San Hup, means three harmonies, three unities, or three combinations, depending on the Mandarin or Cantonese translation. It is considered the oldest form of Classical Feng Shui. The San He School gives great importance and consideration to environmental qualities, such as mountains and topography. The direction, shape, flow, and appearance of these features are important issues to evaluate before the construction of a building or when planning a city. In Neolithic China, Feng Shui was first used to select the ideal location for a home, a village, or an auspicious gravesite for an ancestor. By the Tang Dynasty, Feng Shui had blossomed into a science, sophisticated and complex.

Since San He focuses on the environment—mountains, rivers, and landforms—it strives to understand how the environment shapes and creates chi. San He techniques are focused on finding the most advantageous or strategic location in which to extract the chi from the environment. This school recognizes that chi is dynamic and changes through time. This notion is based on immutable yin energy, such as mountains, to counter fluctuating yang energy, such as time cycles. San He systems do not try to adapt to cycles of chi. Rather, this approach attempts to insulate against and outlive any unfavorable energy cycles by selecting or creating superior landforms.

Figure 52: The San He system's focus is on landforms (natural or human-made) such as roads. Their proximity to the house is very important.

San He also relies on extensive systems and formulas to assess formations for disaster, wealth potential, and good luck. For example, a *Peach Blossom Sha Road* formation indicates bad romance and illicit affairs; an *Eight Roads of Destruction* (Pa Loo Hwang Chuen) causes bankruptcy, divorce, and disaster; and an *Eight Killing Forces* (Pa Sha Hwang Chuen) suggests bad health, money and romance, even murder. Other formulas—such as the *Five Ghost Carry Treasure,* a well-guarded secret from Taiwan, and the *Three Harmony Doorways, He Tu Roads, Assistant Star Water Method, Court Official* and *Sky Horse*—are used to enhance wealth. *Water Dragons* fall under this school and are considered the most powerful of the wealth-producing formulas. There are still other techniques such as the *72 Dragons, 120 Gold Divisions, the 60 Dragons, Triple Goat Punishment, and Six Harms*--all with various methods in analyzing, enhancing or adjusting the Feng Shui of a site.

When it comes to large-scale Feng Shui projects, such as master-planned communities, city planning, high-rise buildings, hotels, resorts, airports, hospitals, and so forth, San He is the best approach. Because this system is so highly developed in landforms—natural and man-made—it excels in methodologies that place the structure in relationship to real and virtual mountains (tall structures) and natural or virtual water (roads). These macro-level considerations should be addressed prior to attempting the micro-engineering design of any structure. But it is perfectly suited for the average home, as well, with numerous techniques that address every area of life.

San Yuan System

Also known as Three Cycles, San Yuan is the contemporary cousin of San He. In San Yuan, chi is understood as dynamic with the disposition to cycle. Nothing in our universe is stagnating; everything is constantly in motion. Even so, it is possible to identify certain dependable trends. That's why it is necessary to regularly update your Feng Shui to stay current with the time cycles of energy. Both San Yuan and San He take into consideration the factors of time and form. The main difference between the two systems is that San He gives great credence to *forms* and San Yuan has an extreme focus on *time*.

Flying Stars explains why no structure will forever enjoy good or bad Feng Shui as it cycles through time. Every structure has its own unique natal Flying Star Chart, which gives vital clues to the distinct energy held there.

Some Flying Star charts are special and indicate exceptional auspiciousness including *Pearl String Formations* (Lin Cu San Poon Gua), *Parent String Formations* (Fu Mo San Poon Gua), and *Combinations of 10*. All three are famous for bringing great money or relationship luck. Other techniques, such as the *Castle Gate Theory* (Sent Mun Kuet), are used to tap the energy of a natural body of water for greater prosperity.

The *Flying Stars system* (Xuan Kong Fei Xing) and *Eight Mansions system* (Pa Chai or Ba Zhai) fall under the major umbrella of the San Yuan School; however Flying Star is specific to Xuan Kong. These are two of the most popular Feng Shui systems used today, especially for interior Feng Shui. In Flying Stars, an energy map of the property is derived from calculations and used to determine the quality of chi in each sector of the home. Eight Mansions, by contrast, is concerned with harmonizing the occupants with the distinctive energies of the house.

Other Feng Shui techniques that fall under the San Yuan and Xuan Kong branches include *Zi Bai* (Purple-White Flying Stars); *Xuan Kong Da Gua* (Big 64 Hexagrams Method), which is used for date selection and *Xuan Kong Shui Fa* (Time-Space Water Method), used to enhance the site through wealth-producing water features. The *Dragon Gate Eight* (Long Men Ba Da Ju) method is part of the San Yuan School and is used to attract wealth and enhance career luck.

The San Yuan system also developed and adopted techniques from the San He School, which assess annual visiting negative energies. The *Three Killings* (Sam Sart), Grand Duke (Tai Sui) and the *Year Breaker* (Sui Po) can cause disastrous outcomes by disturbing the earth with a digging project, such as a pool construction or major landscaping. The annual visit of the *5 Yellow Star* is also disturbed by digging and construction. *The Great Sun Position* (Tai Yang Dou San Pan) is a technique used to counter the effect of these negative energies by selecting a good date to begin your construction or digging project and offers protection from harmful results.

The *Robbery Mountain Sha* (Chor San Kibb Sart) can portend being hurt by knives and serious accidents. The calculation of the daily, monthly and yearly "stars" are other techniques used to assess the Feng Shui and are part of the San Yuan branch of study.

At the end of the day, San He and San Yuan have common denominators. They both agree that the factor of *time* must always be considered and that *landforms* cannot be ignored. Ultimately, San He and San Yuan have one goal: to extract the chi of the environment to support the occupants and enhance the human experience. See the authors other books on these exciting Feng Shui subjects.

The Chinese Luo Pan

Hundreds of years before the Europeans, the ancient Chinese discovered the magnetic compass. The use of the compass for Feng Shui purposes likely pre-dated its maritime use. It seems that the parallel development is of no matter; the Feng Shui compass has always been an instrument of the land not the sea.

There is an intriguing legend about how they acquired this enormous gift as part of their culture—it is the ancient legend of the *Warrior-Goddess of the Nine Heavens*. When China's first ruler, the Yellow Emperor Huangdi (2698 to 2598 BC), was asleep one night, there appeared a bright light from heaven in which the goddess emerged. She held in her hand a 9 by 8-inch jade box. The Yellow Emperor received the jade box from the goddess and found that it contained a magic scroll written on dragon skin. It is said that by following the secrets written on the 'dragon scroll', the Emperor defeated the evil wizard (Chi You) in the famous Battle of Zhuolu.

Thus began the start of the great Han Chinese civilization. Other stories tell about Huangdi's unique invention, a compass cart which leads to victory. Either way, the compass/Luo Pan soon became the quintessential tool of the Feng Shui master.

Throughout its illustrious and long history, the Luo Pan has been redesigned and refined many times over so that it would align with the latest discoveries relating to landforms, techniques, and directional energy. The Luo Pan is an impressive and beautiful instrument, truly a work of art, and well worth the several hundred dollars it commands.

Figure 53: Feng Shui Masters and professional practitioners use a Chinese compass known as a Luo Pan; it is the quintessential tool!

References

Banoo, Sreerema. *How to Use Feng Shui to Help Your Business Succeed: Workplace harmony and good fortune can be attained through the ancient Chinese practice of geomancy.* January 15, 2019. https://www.unreservedmedia.com/feng-shui-business-success/

Better Homes and Garden. August, 2015 https://betterdfw.com/wp-content/uploads/2015/09/Feng-Shui-Survey-Findings-Presentation.pdf

Clarke, Katherine. *Faux pas with foreign buyers From Chinese tax law to Russian commodities, a broker's guide to avoiding cultural pitfalls.* July 01, 2012 https://therealdeal.com/issues_articles/foreign-buyers-101/

Currivan, Jude Ph.D. *The Cosmic Hologram.* Inner Traditions, Rochester, Vermont. 2017.

Jenett, Marilyn. *Feel Free to Pros*per. New York, NY. Penguin Random House. 2015

Johnstone, Debbie. The Arrival of the 818 Light Codes. https://818lightcodes.com

Kane, Colleen. *Ancient art of 'feng shui' is being used to sell luxury real estate.* September 15, 2015 https://fortune.com/2015/09/15/feng-shui-real-estate/

Liotta-Dennis, Denise. *Flying Stars Feng Shui for Period 9.* Moon-Gate Press & KDP. Houston, Texas. 2019.

Losier, Michael J. *Law of Attraction.* New York, NY. Grand Central Publishing, 2003

Murphy, Joseph, Ph.D. *The Power of the Subconscious Mind.* New York, NY, Random House, 2000
        -*Your Infinite Power to Be Rich.* Parker Publishing Company Inc. West Nyack, New Jersey. 1966.

Nelson, Dr. Bradley. *The Emotion Code*. St. Martin's Essentials. New York, NY. 2019. www.DiscoverHealing.com

Pan, Yuqing. *The Lucky Numbers That Can Drive Up Your Home's Value*. Nov 16, 2016 https://www.realtor.com/news/trends/can-lucky-numbers-help-sell-your-home-to-specific-buyers/

Rolando, Donna. *The Eternal Quest for the Perfect Home: More Buyers Turn to Feng Shui Masters for the Answer*. Nov 20, 2018 https://www.realtor.com/news/trends/buyers-check-feng-shui-masters/?mod=article_inline

Schoenberger, Aaron. *Chinese Real Estate Buyers, Feng Shui & Lucky Numbers* Real Estate News Published July 26, 2012

Shinn, Florence Scovel. *The Wisdom of Florence Scovel Shinn* Simon & Schuster Fireside. New York. 1989.

Skinner, Stephen. *Guide to the Feng Shui Compass*. Hoard Press. London, U.K. 2008.

Too, Lillian. *Total Feng Shui, Bring Health, Wealth, and Happiness Into Your Life*. Chronicle Books. San Francisco. 2005.

Van Horebeek, Sam. *Chinese homebuyers say feng shui is imperative*. November 23, 2015 https://www.inman.com/2015/11/23/chinese-homebuyers-say-feng-shui-is-imperative/

Bio of Barbara Harwell (1948-2022)

Feng Shui Master - REALTOR® (TX and AZ) – Teacher – Speaker – Author - Law of Attraction Facilitator - Emotion, Body and Light Code Practitioner - Prayer Chaplain Emeritus

Barbara Harwell is the CEO of *Barbara Harwell International Consultancy,* a global firm that specializes in fully integrated energy solutions.

As a Feng Shui Master, Realtor and natural entrepreneur, Barbara brings over 40-years' experience to her clients. Her father was an entrepreneur who owned various businesses (motel, hardware store, furniture store, ambulance service and mortuary) and held several political leadership positions such as mayor, county judge and city manager. Her expertise in working with homeowners, businesses, investors, corporations, and developers has earned her an incomparable reputation. Ms. Harwell, a native Texan, has owned a commercial real estate company in Texas and a residential real estate company in Arizona. Currently she holds real estate licenses in Texas and Arizona. She is an Arizona Broker Associate, e-Pro® and Certified Real Estate Mentor.

Known as the Feng Shui Deva, she studied with world-renown Grandmaster Lillian Too, the most prolific Feng Shui author based in Kuala Lumpur, Malaysia. Barbara is part of the 400-year Wu Chang Pai lineage of Grandmaster Yap Cheng Hai through her teacher Master Denise Liotta Dennis. Like Denise, she is one of fewer than 100 authentic Feng Shui masters in North America. She is also a Red Ribbon Practitioner with the International Feng Shui Guild (IFSG), past IFSG President of the Phoenix Chapter and Master Instructor for the American College of Classical Feng Shui (ACCFS).

After her near-death experience at age 6, Barbara has had a fascination with all things spiritual and metaphysical. Her interest led her to study with Dr. Ribhi Kalla of the *Ageless Wisdom Seminary University* for many years. She went on to learn The Emotion and Body Code systems with Dr. Bradley Nelson and the Law of Attraction method with famed Michael J. Losier. Barbara uses all her life wisdom and knowledge to bring a comprehensive experience to her clients. They often say they can feel the 'magic' as soon as she steps through the door.

Barbara is the mother of four and grandmother of nine. She lives in Scottsdale, AZ. She has traveled to Europe, Mexico, Malaysia, Canada, Hong Kong and Singapore. Her lifetime education and experiences make her a living treasure and gifted healer.

Contact:
Barbara Harwell International Consultancy
Scottsdale, Arizona USA
480-258-8888 (phone and text)

Connect:
Email: Barbara@BarbaraHarwell.com
Website: BarbaraHarwell.com
Website: FengShuiDeva.com
818 Light Codes: https://818lightcodes.com/

Social Media:
Facebook: https://www.facebook.com/BarbaraHarwell8888
LinkedIn: https://www.linkedin.com/in/barbaraharwellauthor/

Bio of Denise A. Liotta-Dennis

Feng Shui Master, Speaker, Teacher, International Author, Interior Designer, and Home Stager

 **She's known as the "fast-talkin' Texan"** -an interesting and delightful oxymoron. Denise is one of less than 100 genuine Feng Shui masters in North America. With 25+ years of experience, she's the founder and president of *Dragon Gate Feng Shui International Consultants* and *The American College of Classical Feng Shui.* She's been interviewed on television and radio and is the most published Feng Shui author in America.

Born to a Houston entrepreneurial family, Denise, who possesses a quarter century of business ownership experience, is among a rare breed of Feng Shui consultants. Denise not only resonates with all things spiritual, she talks the language and walks in the shoes of business people. Growing up in the shadow of her father's construction and real estate development companies, Denise discovered early in life an innate love of business lifestyles and entrepreneurship. Her work with Feng Shui is also an outgrowth of a natural affinity for interior design. In fact, Denise has more than twenty years' experience working in interior design, including residential and commercial projects.

With a rapid-fire delivery that keeps audiences spellbound, wide-eyed, and on the edge of their seats, Denise—a gifted educator and speaker on Feng Shui and business topics—offers high-energy, content-rich presentations. Peppering her talks with a quaint Southwestern humor, Denise's stories are couched in the real-life foibles of entrepreneurs and those seeking a spiritual path.

She shares the spiritual side of life with a practical commercial bent not found among the more esoteric practitioners common to Feng Shui. Denise has studied with four noted Feng Shui Masters from China, Malaysia and Australia, including Grandmaster Yap Cheng Hai and belongs to his 400- year Wu

Chang Feng Shui Mastery lineage. She has traveled much of the world; South America, Western Europe, Malaysia, Taiwan, Canada, South Africa, Japan and Mexico.

Denise is the author of eight other books which are sold in fine bookstores in the United States, Canada, the United Kingdom, Australia, New Zealand, and Singapore. They are offered online at Walmart, Target, Barnes and Noble, Amazon, and are housed in hundreds of libraries including the *Library of Congress.* International online booksellers in Sweden, Germany, France, Poland, Japan, Italy and Denmark sell her books in English.

Contact:
Dragon Gate Feng Shui International Consultants
The American College of Classical Feng Shui
Houston, Texas USA
713-897-1719 (phone and text)

Connect:
Email: denise@dragongatefengshui.com
Website: www.dragongatefengshui.com
Website: www.RealEstateFengShuiSeries.com

Social Media:
Facebook:
https://www.facebook.com/denise.liottadennis?ref=bookmarks
Twitter: https://twitter.com/deniseannette
LinkedIn: https://www.linkedin.com/pub/denise-liotta-dennis/9/3bb/820

Amazon:
Author Central *(Author's Page on Amazon):*
https://authorcentral.amazon.com/gp/profile

Feng Shui Training Programs

There are several ways to learn more about Feng Shui. The following programs are suitable for real estate agents, architects, Feng Shui enthusiasts, interior designers, self-taught Feng Shui practitioners, builders and Feng Shui professionals seeking to deepen their knowledge, and those aspiring to a career in Feng Shui.

Feng Shui Handbook for Real Estate Agents Certification
Coming Soon!

This *online* training course is an enhanced version of the book. There are a series of ten (10) video modules where Barbara will walk you through learning how to assess properties, take a compass direction, how to implement the recommendations and much, much more! As a BONUS, you will also learn the Eight Mansions system (BaZhai). This is a simple system to learn that produces profound results. You will find the details at www.RealEstateFengShuiSeries.com. You may also contact Barbara@BarbaraHarwell.com or call 480-258-8888.

3-Day Intensive: Professional Certification

In this course you will learn sophisticated techniques to accurately analyze a home or business that will prepare you to be a sought-after consultant. You will learn how to simultaneously use Eight Mansions and Flying Stars, the two most important systems for interiors. Our classes are amazing, exciting and very effective, in just three days you'll know how to apply your new or years of knowledge to create impressive results. Contact Denise at denise@dragongatefengshui.com or 713-897-1719.

3-Day Intensive: Master Certification

The demand for skilled consultants who can produce results has far outstripped the supply. Here you will learn the most advanced techniques of Classical Feng Shui. Experienced practitioners are often hired for large projects for the development of master-planned communities, office buildings, shopping centers, hotels, and casinos. Contact Denise at denise@dragongatefengshui.com or call 713-897-1719

Private Mentoring: FENG SHUI MASTER Program

This is the traditional method of learning Feng Shui mastery and not for everyone. It is a 1-year program (36 Modules) taught twice a month via Skype; Saturday or Sunday is an option if needed. The mentoring program is taught monthly and provides the most personalized, comprehensive program we offer. Contact Denise Liotta-Dennis at denise@dragongatefengshui.com or call 713-897-1719.

Certifications are offered for all the online classes through *The American College of Classical Feng Shui (ACCFS).*

Glossary of Terms

While certainly not an exhaustive directory, it may pique your interest to learn more. This glossary will give you a glimpse of the depth and vibrancy of Feng Shui. As each person's life is improved through Feng Shui its effect reaches out in concentric circles to improve lives globally. Remember, we are all connected, and *everything* is energy. It is time for us all be a part of that positive cycle!

20-Year Period: One of the time increments in the Xuan Kong Fei Xing (Flying Star) system.

24 Mountains: This is the single most important ring on the Chinese Luo Pan/compass. All homes and buildings will be one of these facing directions. Each of the eight directions has three 15° divisions comprising a total of twenty-four equaling a total of 360 degrees. These are indicated in Feng Shui terms as South 1, South 2, South 3 and so forth.

60-Year Cycle: Time cycle encompassing three (3) time Periods.

81 Combinations: The nine Flying Stars paired with each other creating specific outcomes.

Age of Eight: Also known as Period 8. A twenty-year period of time that affects the luck of man and influences the world with its energy. These twenty-year periods were first tracked and recorded by the ancient Chinese in about 2500 BC. They observed that every 180 years the planets in our solar system line up. It was further noted that every twenty years the Milky Way shifts and influences the events of mankind. These periods run from one to nine every twenty years and then start all over again. The current *Age of Eight* began February 4, 2004. This is part of the Flying Star system (Xuan Kong Fei Xing).

Auspicious: Chinese favor the term *auspicious*, meaning something is fortunate or lucky, and good events will ensue.

Ba Gua: Also spelled Pa Kua. An octagonal arrangement of the eight trigrams or Guas of Taoist mysticism that is used as a basic tool of energy assessment in Feng Shui.

Ba Gua Mirror: This mirror (flat, concave, or convex) is surrounded by the eight trigrams and used to deflect negative energy or something in view that is not desirable. This Ba Gua is identified as having three solid lines at the top known as the Chien/Qian trigram or Gua. This is best used sparingly, if at all.

Basements: Traditional basements are built at the sub-ground level and into the earth. They often have small windows looking out on the ground level (dirt or earth). The earth level is cold chi or cold energy.

Bing: One of the 24 Mountain directions; *South 1 Is* between 157.6° to 172.5°.

Black Hat Sect: A new school of Feng Shui brought to the U.S. in the 1980s by Professor Thomas Lin Yun, a Buddhist monk of the Black Hat Order of Tibetan Buddhism (there are also sects that wear red or yellow hats). Although not considered an authentic system of Feng Shui, Black Hat is the most recognized style in the world except in Asian countries, which are most familiar with traditional/classical schools of Feng Shui.

Black Turtle: One of the four Celestial Animals located at the back of your property that serves as support and protection.

Book of Changes: Also known as the *I Ching*.

Bright Hall: This area is an open space near the front door (interior and exterior) where chi can collect; in Chinese known as the *Ming Tang*.

Bull Fight Sha Formation: This combination of the 2 and 3 Flying Stars creates an energy that is conducive for bickering, fighting and marital discord.

Calamity Sha: Another name for the Three Killings formation where it is taboo to engage in deep digging or construction.

Canal: An artificial waterway for boats or irrigation. In Feng Shui, canals are considered rivers; they can be particularly ruinous if they run behind your home.

Cardinal Directions: Points of geographic orientation—North, South, East and West.

Cascading Wind Formation: The 2 and 4 Flying Stars indicating women fighting in the household; usually involving mother-in-law and daughter-in-law.

Castle Gate: A wealth-producing formula in the San Yuan school; the Chinese term is *Cheng Men Jue*. There are actually two popular variations of a Castle Gate.

Central Palace: The center area of a Natal Flying Star Chart.

Celestial Animals: Landforms, natural or man-made that surround and support the occupants of a home or business. In Feng Shui, these are referred to as the Green Dragon, White Tiger, Red Phoenix and Black Turtle. As you are looking out your front door, the left-hand side is the Green Dragon representing male energy; the right-hand side the White Tiger representing female energy; the Red Phoenix is in the front retaining the energy there; and the Black Turtle represents protection at the back.

Chen: One of the 24 Mountain directions; *Southeast 1* is between 112.6° to 127.5°; also represented by the **Dragon**.

Chen: One of the eight trigrams of the Ba Gua. It represents the eldest son, thunder and spring.

Chi: The vital life-force energy of the universe and everything in it; sometimes chi is referred to as *cosmic breath*. It is also spelled *ch'i* or *qi* and is pronounced *chee*.

Chien: Part of the 24 Mountain directions; *Northwest 2* is between 307.6° to 322.5°.

Chien: One of the eight trigrams of the Ba Gua also spelled as *Qian*. It represents the father, the heavens, and late autumn.

Chinese Almanac: Also referred to as the *Tong Shu*. Since ancient times, this annual publication is of great importance to the people of the Orient. It serves as a useful guide to everyday life, dispensing advice on good days for weddings, business transactions and burials. Even in modern times, millions of people still consult the Chinese Almanac every day.

Chinese Animal Zodiac: The **Rat, Ox, Tiger, Rabbit, Dragon, Snake, Horse, Goat/Sheep, Monkey, Rooster, Dog** and **Boar/Pig** represent the Chinese Animal Zodiac which is based on the Lunar calendar. They each appear in a 12-year repeating cycle and each animal sign resides in a specific compass direction.

Chinese Compass: Known as a Luo Pan, it is the quintessential tool of a Feng Shui practitioner. It is a compass that contains four to forty concentric rings of information. The most popular model is approximately ten inches across, square, and often constructed of fine woods. The circle portion of the Luo Pan is made of brass and rotates to align with the compass itself, which is located in the center. There are three major types of Luo Pans—the *San Yuan* Luo Pan, the *San He* Luo Pan, and the *Chung He* Luo Pan (also known as *Zong He* or *Zhung He*), which is a combination of the first two. Though Luo Pans have similar basic components, Feng Shui masters do customize their own with secret information for them and their students.

Chinese Lunar Calendar: A calendar based on the moon cycles.

Chinese Solar Calendar: A calendar based on the rotation of the earth around the sun.

Ching Dynasty: The last ruling dynasty of China; reigned between 1644 and 1912 A.D.

Chou: One of the 24 Mountain directions; *Northeast 1* is between 22.6° to 37.5°; also represented by the **Ox**.

Classical Feng Shui: Also known as Traditional Feng Shui. It is the Feng Shui that has been developed and applied for thousands of years in Asia. Sophisticated forms are practiced in Hong Kong, Taiwan, Malaysia, and Singapore. Classical Feng Shui is just being introduced and practiced in Western countries and is now reaching mainstream status. The traditional systems of Feng Shui are the *San He*, meaning three combinations, and *San Yuan* or three cycles. All techniques, methods, and formulas will be under one or the other. Feng Shui masters and practitioners will use both systems as one comprehensive body of knowledge.

Cold Chi: A room or home built below the earth's surface or into the ground is considered cold chi; these are *yin,* or lifeless environments.

Combination of 10: A wealth-producing chart in the Flying Star system where the Stars add to ten in all nine palaces. In Chinese it is translated as *He Shih Chu.*

Commercial Spaces: Business-related property intended to generate a profit, including shopping centers, office buildings, malls, restaurants, retail shops, boutiques, salons, spas, and hotels.

Construction Date: Many Feng Shui masters in Hong Kong use the date of the building's construction to determine the Period of a Flying Star Chart. Others use "Move-In" date or the date of the most recent substantial remodeling.

Continuous Bead Formation: Another term for the Pearl String Formation; a very special Flying Star chart indicating wealth, and people luck (health, career and relationships).

Cosmic Trinity: Known in Chinese as *Tien-Di-Ren*. Three categories of luck, specifically Heaven Luck, Man (Human) Luck, and Earth Luck. The Chinese believe Heaven Luck is fixed; however, humans have control over personal effort (Man Luck) and Feng Shui (Earth Luck).

DEL - Death and Emptiness Lines: Also known as void, or empty lines, they invite a host of negative events if doors fall on these degrees, which are on the exact Cardinal points, 90, 180, 270, and 360/0. Though other DELs exist on Intercardinal points the consequences are less severe. Void lines are reserved for temples, churches, synagogues, and other places of worship. These degrees can attract or serve as doorways for ghosts or spirits. Also known as *Kong Wang* or *Kun Mang*.

Ding: One of the 24 Mountain directions; *South 3* is between 187.6° to 202.5°.

Direct and Indirect Spirit: This theory restricts the placement of water in four directions in certain Periods. For instance, in Period 6, 7, 8, & 9 it suggests that water can *only* be placed in the North, Southwest, East or Southeast. Southwest would be the 'optimum' position in Period 8 and considered 'direct spirit.' Grandmaster Yap Cheng Hai considers this theory somewhat faulty and not totally accurate. For the most part we do not consider it when placing water. Instead we focus on the overall Feng Shui and activate the wealth Stars (both mountain and water), with the 8 Facing (aka Water) Star getting the foremost consideration. The results have always been excellent.

Double Stars Meet at Facing: *Shuang Xing Dao Xiang* in Chinese means that two stars in the Flying Star system are in the front of the house or building.

Double Stars Meet at Sitting: *Shuang Xing Dao Zuo* in Chinese means that two stars in the Flying Star system are at the back of the house or building.

Dragon: In Feng Shui a Dragon is an undulating mountain. Dragon is also a term used for something powerful or curving, as in the mythical body of a dragon. It can apply to land and water. The Chinese so revere the dragon that it is used in multiple applications and meanings.

Dragon's Vein: The vein of the dragon is an area of chi accumulation, most commonly places of running water. In Feng

Shui, rolling mountains and mountain ranges are called dragons. Where the dragon meets the terrain is its *lair*, or the most powerful spot of a site.

Drain: An opening in the ground usually covered with a grate, which takes water away from an area. In Feng Shui, these are considered *water exits* and can bring wealth or disaster. A drain near a main door of a home or business is always bad. Only exposed drains are important in Feng Shui; underground and invisible formations do not count.

Early Heaven Ba Gua: This is the first arrangement of the eight trigrams; known as the *Ho Tien* or *Fu Xi* Ba Gua in Chinese. It can be easily recognized as the Chien trigram (three solid lines) is always placed on the top.

Earth Luck: One of the three categories of luck that humans can experience. Your luck or good fortune will increase by using Feng Shui, also known as Earth Luck.

Eight Life Stations: Also known as the *Eight Life Aspirations*, these stations correspond to a point on the Ba Gua and an aspect of life such as South - fame; Southwest - marriage; Southeast - wealth; North – career; Northwest – helpful people or mentors, Northeast – skills, knowledge, wisdom, and so forth. This is the product of Black Hat Sect founder Lin Yun. You will sometimes find these referred to by Classical Feng Shui consultants, however, the Eight Life Stations are not found in classic texts nor are they a part of Classical Feng Shui practice and principles.

Electrical Towers: The high-tension towers that bring electricity to an area emit incredibly negative energy. The Swedish government has done extensive research on how these towers affect human beings. Children and the elderly are most vulnerable to this intense energy. Avoid living near these.

Energy: The Chinese call energy chi (also spelled *qi*) and pronounced *chee*. Our entire universe is energy; there are many types of chi including human, environmental, and heaven.

Esoteric: Knowledge that is available only to a narrow circle of enlightened or initiated people or a specially educated group. Feng Shui is part of Chinese metaphysics and is considered esoteric.

External Environment: This covers the terrain and topography, including mountains, water, and other natural formations. It also encompasses man-made features, such as roads, pools, retaining walls, highways, poles, drains, washes, tall buildings, stop signs, fire hydrants, and other structures.

Facing Direction: The front side of the home or building, generally where the front or main door is located and faces the street. When a door is on the side of the house or is angled, the Facing direction is determined by standing at the front and center of the structure facing the street. There are some instances where other methods are used to establish the Facing Direction.

Facing Star: Also known as the Water Star, it is always activated by actual water or movement such as doors opening, etc. This star is located in the upper right-hand corner of a Flying Star chart in all nine palaces or sectors. The Facing Star is in charge of wealth luck. In Chinese it is known as *Shui Xing*.

Feng Shui: Also known as *Kan Yu* (translated as *the way of heaven and earth*) until about a hundred years ago. It is the Chinese system of maximizing the accumulation of beneficial chi which improves the quality of life and luck of the occupants of a building or location. Pronounced *fung shway or foong shway*.

Feng Shui Master: One who has mastered the skills of Classical Feng Shui and/or has been declared as such by his or her teacher, or both. It is also said that a practitioner becomes a master when his or her clients refer to them as master. Most Feng Shui masters from classic traditions will belong to a lineage of their teachers. This is also known as *a lineage carrier,* meaning the master carries on the teachings and practices of his or her education. A Feng Shui master generally oversees his or her own school and students, too.

Feng Shui Schools: There are two major schools (not physical locations, rather they are systems) of Classical Feng Shui, San He and San Yuan; hundreds of formulas, techniques, and systems serve as subsets of either school. If you practice Classical Feng Shui, you use the San He and the San Yuan systems as one extensive body of knowledge.

Fire Burning Heaven's Gate: The Northwest location of your site is known as 'heaven's gate'. The Flying Star 6 also represents the heavens. When there is the real element of fire, such as a stove or kitchen, in the Northwest sector of the house, it is said that 'fire is burning heaven's gate". This can also happen when the 9 star and the 6 star (of the Flying Star system) come together in *any* palace but is considered seriously inauspicious when these stars are present in the Northwest palace. Either the star combination (9–6) or, the presence of real fire in the Northwest always brings bad luck to the father, president, or the leader.

Five Elements: *Wu Xing* in Chinese; the five elements are wood, fire, earth, metal and water. There are three important cycles which are *producing, reducing* and *controlling*. They are used as valuable Feng Shui enhancements and cures.

Floating Stars: Another name for the Flying Stars found in the book *The Complete Idiot's Guide to Feng Shui.*

Flying Stars: Known as *Xuan Kong Fei Xing* in Chinese, which means *mysterious void* or the *subtle mysteries of time and space.* It is a popular Feng Shui system that is superior in addressing the time aspect of energy. While there are only 9 Flying Stars, when paired they create 81 combinations. When activated properly or cured when necessary they produce powerful results.

Fu Mo San Poon Gua: Very special Flying Star chart also called the Parent String Formation. In each palace/sector, three numbers must be present 3-6-9, 2-5-8 and 1-4-7.

Fu Xi: A sage, king and shaman who was responsible for discovering and arranging the Early Heaven Ba Gua.

Gen: One of the 24 Mountain directions; *Northeast 2* is between 37.6° to 52.5°.

Gen: One of the eight trigrams of the Ba Gua also spelled as *Ken*. It represents the youngest son, the mountain and early spring.

Geng: One of the 24 Mountain directions; *West 1* is between 247.6° to 262.5°.

Geomancy: The word geomancy means divination or foresight by the earth. It is sometimes incorrectly used as a connotation for Feng Shui. Geomancy is an Arabic system of divination having its origins in North Africa during the 9th century.

Grand Duke Jupiter: The Tai Sui aka Grand Duke is "seated with" the reigning animal of the year. For example, in 2020 the Grand Duke is located in North 2, the home of the Rat.

Grandmaster of Feng Shui: Person who has been practicing and teaching Feng Shui for many years, belongs to a respected lineage of masters, and has at least one master among his or her pupils.

Great Cycle: Represents the nine Periods multiplied by 20 years which is the length of each Period. Great Cycles last for 180 years. Also see *Age of Eight* in this Glossary of Terms.

Green Dragon: A Celestial Animal that represents the left side of your property as you look out the front door.

Gua: Also spelled *Kua* and also known as a trigram. It represents one of eight Guas of the Ba Gua, defined by a combination of three solid or broken lines.

Hai: One of the 24 Mountain directions; *Northwest 3 is* between 322.6° to 337.5° degrees; also represents the **Boar/Pig**.

He Shih Chu: Very special Flying Star chart of the *Combination of Ten* in which the Stars in all 9 palaces/sectors add to 10. There are two types of charts; when the Stars add to 10 towards the Facing (Water) Star, it indicates great wealth. When the Stars add to 10 towards the Mountain Star, people luck is indicated such as health, career, relationships and so forth.

Heaven Luck: One of the three categories of luck that humans can experience. The Chinese believe every human arrives on earth with a God-given fate. This category is considered *fixed* while Human Luck and Earth Luck can be influenced.

Heavenly Heart: Is the central palace of the Luo Shu (*magic square of 15)* and the center of the home or building. Sometimes spelled *Lo Shu*.

Hexagrams: Are the eight trigrams stacked one on top of another—creating 64 possible combinations. The hexagrams are the foundation of the I Ching.

High-rise Building: In the external environment, high-rise buildings and skyscrapers function as *virtual* or *urban mountains*.

Ho Hai: Also known as *Wo Hai*. Part of the Eight Mansions system and can bring mishaps—nothing goes smoothly.

Houseboat: This type of dwelling is popular in certain parts of the world. Living on a boat creates instability—a foundation on water is precarious. Money and health will always be issues.

I Ching: A philosophical and divinatory book based on the sixty-four hexagrams of Taoist mysticism. It is also known as the *Classic of Changes* or *Book of Changes*.

I Ching Feng Shui: Also known as *Xuan Kong Da Gua*. A San Yuan system of Feng Shui that relies on the sixty-four hexagrams of the *I Ching*. Often referred to as the Big 64 Hexagrams, this method offers various techniques—the most popular is the auspicious date selection for important events.

Incoming Dragon: The energy of a mountain that comes directly to your home or building. If a mountain range is nearby, the highest peak is measured with a Luo Pan because it has the most powerful energy. An entire science is based on determining the effects of mountain energy on any given site. In Feng Shui, mountains and dragons are used interchangeably.

Interior Environment: The interior environment encompasses anything that falls within the walls of a structure, including kitchen, staircase, master bedroom, fireplaces, bathrooms, hallways, dining room, bedrooms, appliances, furniture, and so on.

Intercardinal Directions: Northwest, Southwest, Northeast and Southeast.

Jia: Part of the 24 Mountain directions; *East 1* is between 67.6° to 82.5°.

Kan: One of the eight trigrams. It represents the middle son, the moon and mid-winter.

Kong: Emptiness, void, form or space.

Kong Wang: Also known as Kun Mang, they are void lines or Death and Emptiness Lines (DEL); they invite a host of negative events if doors are facing these degrees. See also DEL.

Kun: One of the 24 Mountain directions; *Southwest 2* is between 217.6° to 232.5°.

Kun: One of the eight trigrams. It represents the mother, the earth and late summer.

Kwei: One of the 24 Mountain directions; *North 3* is between 7.6° to 22.5°.

Later Heaven Ba Gua: The second arrangement of the trigrams known as the *Wen Wang* or *Xien Tien* Ba Gua. This is used extensively in the application of Classical Feng Shui.

Li: One of the eight trigrams. It represents the middle daughter, fire and full summer.

Li Chun: The day the annual Flying Star changes; the beginning of the Chinese Solar New Year on February 3, 4th or 5th.

Lillian Too: Feng Shui Grandmaster and MBA Harvard Graduate who lives in Kuala Lumpur, Malaysia. She has also written over 200 Feng Shui books, translated into 30 languages, with sales of more than 10,000,000 copies. In the last 25 years, she has built a Feng Shui empire along with her daughter Jennifer. Grandmaster Too learned Feng Shui from Grandmaster Yap Cheng Hai, who also collaborated with her on her earlier books including the famous *Water Feng Shui for Wealth* about water dragons.

Lin Cu San Poon Gua: Very special Flying Star chart—that of the *Pearl String* or *String of Pearls Formation*. In each palace/sector, the numbers will run in a sequence (e.g. 3, 4, 5 or 1, 2, 3). There are two types of Pearl Stings; if the numbers run in sequence towards the facing (aka water) Star, then it will bring wealth-luck. If the numbers run towards the Mountain Star, it will bring people luck (career, relationships, health and so on).

Lineage: The line of transmission of sacred knowledge from a common ancestor who is deemed the founder.

Literary Formation: When the 1 and 4 Flying Stars combine in the same palace or sector of the house.

Ling Xing: The period/time star of a Flying Star chart.

Location: A particular place or position, differing from the concept of *direction*. For example, your living room might be located on the South side of your home (location), but your desk faces North (direction).

Long Chi: Energy that runs along an extended road or pathway.

Lunar Calendar: A calendar based on the cycles of the moon.

Luo Pan aka Luo Jing: This is the quintessential tool of a Feng Shui practitioner. It is a compass that contains four to forty concentric rings of information. The most popular model is approximately ten inches across, square, and often constructed of fine woods. The circle part of the Luo Pan is made of brass and rotates to align with the compass itself, which is located in the center. There are three major types of Luo Pans—the *San Yuan* Luo Pan, the *San He* Luo Pan, and the *Chung He* Luo Pan (also known as *Zong He* or *Zhung He*), which is a combination of the first two. Though Luo Pans have similar basic components, Feng Shui masters do customize their own with secret information for themselves and their students.

Luo Shu: A square that contains nine palaces or cells with a number in each; it adds to fifteen in any direction. The Luo Shu is also known as the *Magic Square of 15* because the sum of the numbers in each palace is 15. Sometimes spelled Lo Shu.

Mao: One of the 24 Mountain directions; *East 2* is between 82.6° to 97.5°; also represented by the **Rabbit**.

Main Door: This is usually the front door of the home or business. If the occupants always enter the residence from the garage, this may also be considered a main door.

Man Luck or Human Luck: One of the three categories of luck that a human can experience. This area of fortune is mutable and defined by individual effort, such as hard work, study, education, experience and good deeds.

Menacing Formation: When the 2 and 5 Flying Stars combine together they can cause all types of disasters.

Ming Dynasty: A ruling dynasty of China, which lasted from 1368 to 1644.

Ming Tang: Means 'bright hall' and is usually an open courtyard or open space near the entrance where chi/energy is able to collect.

Mountain Star: Also known as the Sitting Star. This star is located in the upper left-hand corner of a Flying Star chart in all nine palaces or sectors. It is the Flying Star that is activated by actual or virtual mountains such as statues, boulders, bookcases, walls, etc. that are at least 3 feet tall. It is in charge of people and relationship luck of all kinds. In Chinese it is known as *Shui Xing*.

Mountains: Includes real mountains and virtual mountains, such as tall buildings, landscape mounds, retaining walls, huge boulders, or any object of mass in the environment.

Move-In Date: This is the actual date someone moves into a home or office. Many Feng Shui masters and consultants find this the most accurate method to determine the Flying Star chart for a property.

Parent String Formation: Known in Chinese as *Fu Mu San Poon Gua* and sometimes referred to as the *Three Combinations*, these are special wealth-producing Flying Star charts. This formation of energy applies to certain structures—which are activated by a mountain in the front of the property and water in the back—on intercardinal directions. They only last for twenty years and are unlucky if not activated properly.

Pearl String Formation: Known in Chinese as *Lin Cu San Poon Gua* and sometimes referred to as the *Continuous Bead Formations*. These are special wealth-producing Flying Star charts that only show up in homes that face an intercardinal direction. Though excellent energy for prosperity, this formation only lasts for twenty years and is unlucky if not activated properly.

Period: The twenty-year increment of the Flying Star system; the world is in Period 8 until February 3, 2024. Nine periods comprise a megacycle of 180 years. Period 8 has served to exposes untruths and things once hidden. Period 9 will usher in a more spiritual energy much like going from darkness into light.

Prosperous Sitting and Facing: Known in Chinese as *Wang Shan Wang Shui*. A Flying Star chart that means *good for people, good for money*. These charts have the perfect placement of the current prosperous stars—the Facing (Water) Star is at the facing (good for money), and the Mountain Star is at the sitting (good for people).

Qi Men Dun Jia: The *Mysterious Doorway Hidden Jia (to a Thriving Kingdom)*; this technique is known by many different names throughout history and is an advanced metaphysical secret that was reserved by kings and generals in ancient China.

Red Phoenix: A Celestial Animal that represents the front of your property; also known as *Vermillion Bird*.

Ren: One of the 24 Mountain directions; *North 1* is between 337.6° to 362.5°.

Retaining Walls: High walls, at least three feet in height, which can be used to secure a site and prevent loss of energy. The more severe the landscape, the more walls are needed to protect sloping areas or sharp drop-offs.

Road: A route, path, or open way for vehicles. In Feng Shui, roads are *rivers* of energy, or chi and play a huge part in analyzing a site because energy is powerful. These virtual, or urban, rivers are calculated when assessing, designing, enhancing, or implementing counter measures or enhancements for a site. Having a road or any *river* of energy behind yourself can create unfortunate events.

Sam Sart: The *Three Killings* is an energetic affliction that changes positions each year and only resides in Cardinal directions. Other common names are San Sha (Mandarin), Sam Sart (Cantonese), Sarm Sart, Jupiter Calamity, Sui Sart, Kibb Sart and Coy Sart. The area should be kept quiet during the year that it occupies that specific compass direction. When construction is necessary in the 3 Killings area there are certain days that should be observed so that this affliction is not disturbed.

San He: Also known as *San Hup*. One of the two major schools of study in Classical Feng Shui—the other is San Yuan. The San He system, excellent for tapping natural landforms, primarily addresses large-scale projects, land plots, urban developments, city planning, and master-planned communities.

The system is extensive and has several practical techniques for new and existing residential spaces as well. When assessing and altering a site or a structure, San He and San Yuan can be blended for maximum results.

San Yuan: One of the two major schools of Classical Feng Shui. The Flying Stars is part of this system; it excels in techniques of timing.

Sector: An area inside or outside a building: South sector, North sector, Southeast sector, Northwest sector, and so on.

Sha Chi: Also known as *shar chi*. Extremely negative energy or killing chi.

Shan Xing: The Chinese name of the Mountain (Sitting) Star of a Flying Star chart.

Shui Xing: Means the Water/Facing Star of a Flying Star chart.

Shen: One of the 24 Mountain directions; *Southwest 3* is between 232.6° to 247.5°; also represents the **Monkey**.

Sin/Xin: One of the 24 Mountain directions; *West 3* is between 277.6° to 292.5°.

Su/Si: One of the 24 Mountain directions; *Southeast 3* is between 142.6° to 157.5°; represented by the **Snake**.

Sitting: In Feng Shui it refers to the back of the house, as if the structure is sitting in a chair on the land or property.

Sitting Star: Also known as the Mountain Star in the Flying Star system. It influences people and relationship luck, such as fertility, employees, and health.

Solar Calendar: A calendar based on the movements of the sun.

Southeast Asia: Countries south of China and east of India, including Thailand, Malaysia, Vietnam, Cambodia, Laos,

Brunei, Myanmar (Burma), Indonesia, Timor-Leste, the Philippines, and Singapore.

Squeezed Chi: A phenomenon that happens when a building is extremely narrow and does not allow chi to flow or expand. It will deplete wealth and create debt.

Tai Chi: The black and white symbol of Taoist philosophy; a sphere with two semi-circles intertwined showing the division of yin and yang energy.

Tao: Also known as *The Way*, and is core of Taoism (pronounced with a *D* sound, as in *Dow*).

Tan Lang: The collection of the nine Flying Stars and also known as the *lesser wandering stars* or *small wandering sky*.

Tapping the Energy or Chi: A technique that invites the available energy from the external environment to support the occupants of a structure.

Three Killings: Also known as *Sam Sart* in Chinese. This negative energy visits a different direction annually. Digging into the earth can disturb this energy and can bring on calamity, that's why it is also referred to as *calamity sha*.

Tilting a Door: A time-honored tradition used by Feng Shui masters and practitioners to change the degree of a door and the energy of a space. The doorframe and threshold are re-angled toward the desired degree. When the door is re-hung, it is tilted to a different compass direction degree and is used to identify a different Flying Star chart than existed prior to the tilt.

Tzi/Zi: One of the 24 Mountain directions; *North 2* is between 352.6° to 7.5°; also represented by the **Rat**.

Time Star: Also known as the *Base or Natal Star* in the Flying Star system; it is the single star below the Mountain/Sitting and Water/Facing Star of the chart.

Ting/Ding: One of the 24 Mountain directions; *South 3* is between 187.6° to 202.5°.

T-Juncture: When two roads meet perpendicularly to create a *T*. The formation is toxic when a home or business sits at the top and center of that *T*.

Traditional Feng Shui: Another term for Classical Feng Shui.

Tui: Also spelled *Dui*. One of the eight trigrams that represents the youngest daughter, the lake, and mid-fall.

Up the Mountain, Down the River: Also known as *Shang Shan Xia Shui* in Chinese. The prominent Stars of the period are in reversed positions.

Virtual Mountains: High-rise structures, such as apartments, office buildings, and skyscrapers, are considered virtual or urban mountains and will influence the energy of nearby structures accordingly.

Virtual Water: Roads, sidewalks, driveways, low ground, highways, and other similar formations that are purveyors of chi.

Wang Shan Wang Shui: Means the Star Chart is lucky for money and lucky for people.

Water: In Feng Shui, water is the secret to enhancing wealth, prosperity, longevity and nobility. The Chinese word is *Shui,* representing energy and life force. Water, according to Feng Shui, is the most powerful element on the planet.

Water Exits: The location or direction where water leaves a site. Water exits are used in Feng Shui to bring good results, but if they are not placed well, disaster can ensue.

Waterfalls: Used to enhance wealth luck; the direction of the waterfall flow is important.

Water Star: Also called the *Facing Star* in the Flying Star system. It is in charge of wealth luck.

Wei: One of the 24 Mountain directions; *Southwest 1* is between 202.6° to 217.5°; also represented by the **Goat/Sheep**.

Western Feng Shui: In addition to the Black Hat Sect, other schools have cropped up that incorporated the principles, but not the rituals, associated with Lin-Yun's followers. As the masters of Classical Feng Shui started to teach around the world, some of the most well-acclaimed instructors and authors of Western Feng Shui began to learn Classical Feng Shui. Unwilling to give up the Western-style Feng Shui that made them famous, they mixed the old with the new, thereby adding to the confusion over authentic Feng Shui. More than half of the Feng Shui books written about the subject include a mixture of both theories.

White Tiger: The celestial animal that represents the right-hand side of your property as you look out your front door.

Wu: One of the 24 Mountain directions; *South 2* is between 172.6° to 187.5° degrees; also represented by the **Horse**.

Wu Chang Pai: A Feng Shui lineage dating back 400 years.

Wu Xing: Also known as the five elements of Feng Shui: wood, fire, earth, metal, and water.

Yang: Alive, active and moving energy; considered the male energy of the Yin-Yang symbol.

Yang Feng Shui: Originally Yin Feng Shui was practiced for auspicious gravesite selection. Later, techniques were developed to increase luck and opportunities for houses of the living which is referred to as Yang Feng Shui.

Year Breaker: Location of the direct opposite direction to the Grand Duke which changes annually. Also known as Sui Po.

Yi: One of the 24 Mountain directions; *East 3* is between 97.6° to 112.5°.

Yin: One of the 24 Mountain directions; *Northeast 3 is* between 52.6° to 67.5° degrees; also represented by the **Tiger**.

Yin: Female energy that is passive; the perfect complement is yang energy which is male and active.

You: One of the 24 Mountain directions; *West 2 is* between 262.6° to 277.5°; also represented by the **Rooster**.

Xin: One of the 24 Mountain directions; *West 3*

Xing Fa: An approach to assessing form and shape in the Glossary of **Xu:** One of the 24 Mountain directions; *Northwest 1 is* between 292.6° to 307.5° degrees; also represented by the **Dog**.

Yuan: 60 years.

Xun/Sun: One of the 24 Mountain directions; *Southeast 2* is between 127.6° to 142.5°.

Xun: One of the eight trigrams of the Ba Gua also spelled as *Sun*. It represents the eldest daughter, the wind and early summer.

Classical Feng Shui for Wealth & Abundance
By Master Denise Liotta Dennis
ISBN 978-0-7387-3353-1
$17.99

Unlock the full wealth potential of your home or office using the potent formulas and wisdom of Classical Feng Shui. Written by a Feng Shui master, *Classical Feng Shui for Wealth & Abundance* reveals authentic techniques for success with money, business, and career. In this book, beginners and advanced students will learn:

- The two most popular Feng Shui systems: Eight Mansions and Flying Stars
- Easy-to-use Get Rich Keys and your personal Life Gua number for money luck
- Wealth building formulas such as Five Ghosts Carry Treasure, Dragon Gate, and Water Dragons
- How to identify and eliminate killing chi like Eight Roads of Destruction, Robbery Mountain Sha, and Eight Killing Forces

Whether you're buying a house, creating a home, or managing a business, these ancient and powerful techniques are exactly what you need to capture prosperity and success.

Available at BarnesandNoble.com, Amazon.com and lewellyn.com.
Also available at Barnes & Noble brick and mortar locations.

Classical Feng Shui for Romance, Sex & Relationships
By Master Denise Liotta Dennis
ISBN 978-0-7387-4188-8
$19.99

Harness the ancient power and wisdom of Classical Feng Shui to enhance all your relationships, from romantic pursuits to day-to-day interactions with friends, family, and coworkers. Explore real-life stories of men and women's struggles with love and relationships and how Feng Shui enabled them to overcome their obstacles. Whether you are a beginner or advanced student, Master Denise Liotta Dennis provides you with step-by-step instructions on:

- The two most popular Feng Shui systems: Eight Mansions and Flying Stars
- How to heal your house of detrimental formations that will repel romance and cause negative relationships
- Never-before-seen insights on the Life Gua Zodiac, which helps you assess personality matches

Classical Feng Shui for Romance, Sex & Relationships is filled with effective methods for attracting love, prosperity, and even your soul mate. Use this comprehensive guide to improve not just the energy of your living space today, but also your happiness for many years to come.

Available at BarnesandNoble.com, Amazon.com and lewellyn.com.
Also available at Barnes & Noble brick and mortar locations.

Classical Feng Shui for Health, Beauty & Longevity
By Master Denise Liotta Dennis
ISBN 978-0-7387-4900-6
$21.99

Improve your wellness, extend your longevity, and secure a healthy environment with the ancient power and wisdom of Classical Feng Shui. This comprehensive guide reveals ancient and modern techniques for lasting health and beauty that both beginners and advanced students can use. Providing step-by-step instruction, Feng Shui Master Denise Liotta Dennis teaches you:

- The two most popular Classical Feng Shui systems: Flying Stars and Eight Mansions
- Feng Shui's Taoist roots and a variety of health modalities from ancient and modern times
- Profound secrets of the "Heavenly Doctor" position and its importance in enhancing health
- Ways to protect your body and mind from detrimental formations, devices, and environments

With well-researched information, period charts, astoundingly accurate health predictions, and much more, *Classical Feng Shui for Health, Beauty & Longevity* will help you be happier and healthier. P*raise:* "Denise Liotta Dennis has done a great job of clearly expressing [the application of feng shui to health], going into great detail."—Grand Master Dr. Stephen Skinner

Available at BarnesandNoble.com, Amazon.com and Llewellyn.com.
It can also be purchased at Barnes & Noble brick and mortar locations.
This book is offered in English, Czech and Estonian translations.

Feng Shui That Rocks the House
By Master Denise Liotta Dennis
ISBN-13: 978-1986762892
$28.95

This book explains how to use the simple, yet profound Eight Mansions system. It is a more personalized Feng Shui. Learn your own Magic Life Gua number and unlock the mysteries to a better life. While it is a compass-based formula, it is easy, effective and powerful. Designed to improve relationships, health and prosperity, you will learn the secrets passed down from Grandmaster Yap Cheng Hai from the famous Golden Star Classics. This book will teach you how to 'rock' your home and business—and finally get the life you want! *You will learn:*

How to Calculate Magic Life Gua Numbers

Your Four Good Directions + Your Four Bad Directions

Where to Locate your Marital Bed + How to Improve Romance and Love

How to Jump Start Career Luck

Where to Place Students to Pass Exams

Life Gua Zodiac Personalities + Life Gua Compatibility (64 Combos)

How Fire Affects Money, Relationships & Health

How Doors Activate Specific Types of Luck + The Famous Golden Star Classics

Available at BarnesandNoble.com and Amazon.com

Hollywood's Fatal Feng Shui
By **Master Denise Liotta Dennis** & **Master Jennifer Bonetto**
ISBN-13:978-1986981965
$29.95

This is the first book to do a critical assessment of the tragic homes of Marilyn Monroe, Michael Jackson, O.J. Simpson, Nicole Brown Simpson, Phil Hartman, Anna Nicole Smith, Sharon Tate, Phil Spector, Lyle and Erik Menendez, and Brittany Murphy using Feng Shui. These famous Hollywood stories still haunt us today. These celebrities' homes attracted illicit affairs, drug abuse, lawsuits, murder, sexual scandals, greed, bankruptcy, cult-driven murders, loss of reputation, and fatal illness.

Feng Shui can explain why the energy of these gorgeous properties created the perfect storm and turned their lives upside down! The book took over a year of digging through public records locating accurate floor plans and land surveys. Along with other research, this allowed for a comprehensive assessment of each property. Classical Feng Shui systems, formulas and methods are explained so the reader may appreciate how it *all* went so wrong. You'll learn about disastrous formations such as the Peach Blossom Sha (illicit affairs, fatal attractions), Eight Roads of Destruction/Hell (bankruptcy, divorce), Eight Mountain Killing Forces (murder and crimes of passion), Robbery Mountain Sha (being hurt by knives), deadly Flying Star combinations and much, much more.

Available at BarnesandNoble.com and Amazon.com

How to Start and Grow a Feng Shui Business
By Master Denise Liotta Dennis
ISBN 13: 978-1726468718
$19.95

How to Start and Grow a Feng Shui Business is for Classical Feng Shui practitioners and professionals who desire to begin their studies, near completing or have completed. The first book of its type to guide you in every aspect of creating a successful consulting business. Some topics discussed:

- How to conduct an assessment step-by-step
- Generating a professional report and delivering results
- Classical Feng Shui cures and enhancements
- Fees, checklist, charts, and more
- How to generate a constant flow of clients
- Lecturing to realtors, interior designers and other groups
- Sample Feng Shui reports
- Creating a brand and marketing materials
- Going public—TV, Radio Talk Shows, Vlogging and YouTube videos
- Writing books and blogging
- Organizing a professional consulting book
- Adjunct services you could offer—home staging, BaZi, date selection, interior design, real estate, architecture, or remodeling
- 100+ photos of Denise's studies with Grandmaster Yap in Germany, Malaysia, South Africa and Sedona

Purchase this book at BarnesandNoble.com and Amazon.com

The Secrets to Mastering Flying Stars Feng Shui
By Master Denise Liotta Dennis
ISBN-13: 978-1985760127
$38.95

Flying Stars is the most popular, intriguing and misunderstood Feng Shui system in the world. Whether you're a practitioner or a novice, you'll be able to master and deepen your understanding of a method used for 'superior living'. This book delivers a detailed explanation of how *time* and *space* will affect all categories of Feng Shui, that of prosperity, relationships and health.

A fully illustrated, comprehensive and systematic home-study course that is designed for anyone who wants to put Flying Stars Feng Shui to personal, professional or practical use. With over 20 years' experience, Master Liotta Dennis reveals the best tricks-of-the-trade. Step by step you are guided to shake up the energy and make-over your home or office while simultaneously learning the profound secrets of Flying Stars.

Purchase this book at BarnesandNoble.com and Amazon.com

Flying Stars Feng Shui for Period 9
By Master Denise Liotta Dennis
ISBN-9781983872242
$29.99

Period 9, the *Age of Fire,* will begin on Feb 4, 2024. This is a capital change for all structures worldwide. It will be a time of great intellectual leaps, accomplishments, technology, and a future filled with bright prosperity! It is an 'age' for women.

Flying Stars Feng Shui for Period 9 reveals all you need to know in order to prepare for this incredible and auspicious time. Flying Stars is a potent method of Feng Shui that addresses the time transformation of chi. This changing flow of energy is expressed as numbers in a Flying Star Chart. Worldwide, this capital change happens every 20 years. Therefore, slight adjustments to your home or office need to take place. This exciting, subtle, and important aspect of Feng Shui is the focus of the book.

Flying Stars is the most popular Classical Feng Shui system used by practitioners today. This is because it has a potent effect on properties where it is used. Feb 4, 2024 marks the date when Period 8 ends and Period 9 begins. This book will explain the significant implications of a Period change.

Purchase this book at BarnesandNoble.com and Amazon.com

Eight Mansions Zodiac Feng Shui
By Master Denise Liotta Dennis
ISBN: 9798559412320
$19.99

Whether you're looking for love or that great job/promotion, *Eight Mansions Zodiac Feng Shui* will give you insights as how to capitalize on these opportunities. The Eight Mansions system (BaZhai) is rich in detail and when combined with the Chinese Zodiac animals, will give you a more comprehensive experience. Just by examining your Life Gua Number and animal year of birth, you can be prepared in life regarding your health, career, romance, relationship compatibility and wealth prospects. This book includes even *more* and the following:

- · The 12 Chinese Zodiac Animals
- · 56 Life-Gua Zodiac Personalities
- · The 8 Life-Gua Magic Number
- · 64 Compatibilities for Romance/Marriage
- · Compatibility in the Workplace
- · Your Personal Power Direction
- · Life-Guas +the 5 Elements

Start today improving romance,/relationships family life, work opportunities, selecting the right business partner, and self-awareness!

Purchase this book at Amazon.com

Flying Stars Feng Shui for 2021
By Master Denise Liotta Dennis
ISBN: 9798653215704
$29.95

Flying Stars Feng Shui for 2021 will show you how to powerfully extract the Annual & Monthly stars with House Charts. No book to date has revealed the real secrets and methods of the yearly and monthly stars! **2021** is the *Year of the Ox* and the stars indicate that, unlike the previous year, it's a time of harmony and peace. The Ox energy indicates reconstruction--economically, emotionally and spiritually. We get to hit the restart button! Those born in the Year of Ox, Snake or Rooster will be particularly influenced, however everyone can benefit.

> Annual & Monthly charts for 2021-2030
>
> How to Activate the Facing & Mountain stars
>
> 4 MasterClass techniques to evaluating the stars (Annual+ Monthly+ Facing)
>
> Cures and Enhancements
>
> The Eight Different Types of Flying Star Charts
>
> How Energy Gets Triggered for the Year
>
> How to Treat the 5 Yellow Star
>
> Three Killings, Grand Duke, Year Breaker
>
> The Great Sun Formula+ Waxing Moon Dates
>
> Over 50 pages of Detailed Assessments

Purchase this book at Amazon.com

Made in the USA
Monee, IL
13 March 2024

54965098R00132